IRELAND

THE BRITANNICA GUIDE TO COUNTRIES OF THE EUROPEAN UNION

IRELAND

EDITED BY JEFF WALLENFELDT, MANAGER, GEOGRAPHY

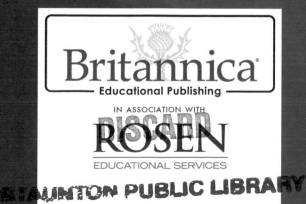

Britannica
Educational Publishing

IN ASSOCIATION WITH

ROSEN
EDUCATIONAL SERVICES

Published in 2014 by Britannica Educational Publishing
(a trademark of Encyclopædia Britannica, Inc.)
in association with Rosen Educational Services, LLC
29 East 21st Street, New York, NY 10010.

First Edition

Britannica Educational Publishing
J.E. Luebering: Director, Core Reference Group
Adam Augustyn: Assistant Manager, Core Reference Group
Marilyn L. Barton: Senior Coordinator, Production Control
Steven Bosco: Director, Editorial Technologies
Lisa S. Braucher: Senior Producer and Data Editor
Yvette Charboneau: Senior Copy Editor
Kathy Nakamura: Manager, Media Acquisition
Jeff Wallenfeldt, Manager, Geography and History

Rosen Educational Services
Hope Lourie Killcoyne: Executive Editor
Nelson Sá: Art Director
Karen Huang: Photo Researcher
Brian Garvey: Designer, Cover Design
Introduction by Hope Lourie Killcoyne

Library of Congress Cataloging-in-Publication Data

Ireland/edited by Jeff Wallenfeldt.—First edition.
    pages cm.—(The Britannica guide to countries of the European Union)
Includes bibliographical references and index.
ISBN 978-1-62275-058-0 (library binding)
1. Ireland—Juvenile literature. 2. Ireland—History—Juvenile literature. I. Wallenfeldt,
Jeffrey H.
DA906.I727 2013
941.5—dc23

        2013006130

Manufactured in the United States of America

On the cover: The National Conference Centre on the River Liffey in Ireland's capital,
Dublin, is seen behind the harp-like Samuel Becket Bridge, named for the famed Irish
author, critic, and playwright. *Trish Punch/Lonely Planet Images/Getty Images* (Samuel
Beckett bridge), *Peter Zoeller/Design Pics/Perspectives/Getty Images* (Convention Centre).

Cover, p. iii (map and stars), back cover, multiple interior pages (stars) ©iStockphoto.
com/pop_jop; cover, multiple interior pages (background graphic) Mina De La O/Digital
Vision/Getty Images

CONTENTS

76

94

96

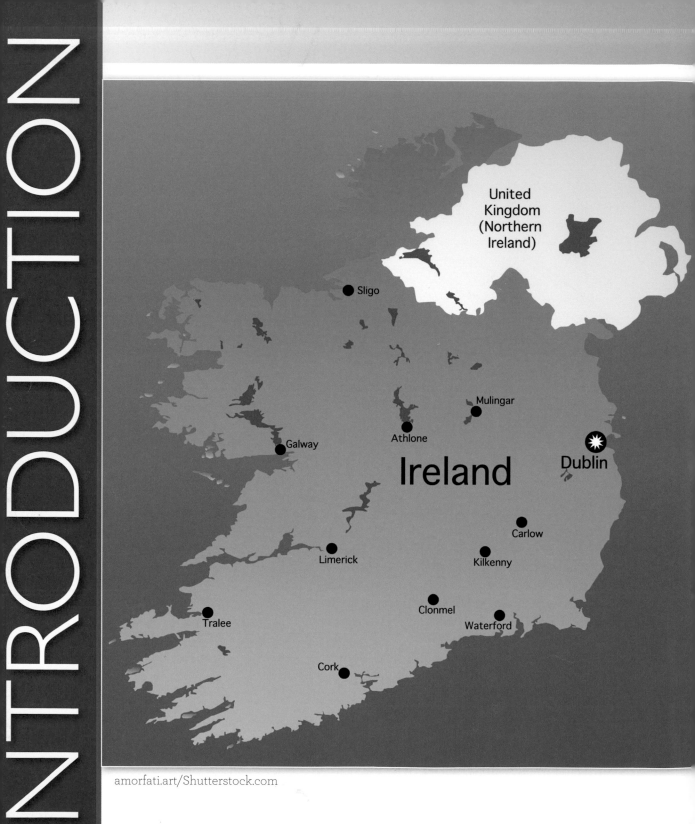

The story of Ireland's history might be thought of as a tale of two pities: the pity of a thousand years' worth of domination of the Emerald Isle, first by the Vikings and then most notably by the English, the latter with its occasional bloody slaughters and debasement of much of Ireland's inhabitants; as well as the pity of struggles and battles among the Irish themselves, which most often, but not always, occurred along religious lines between Roman Catholics and Protestants.

And though one would not and *should* not in good conscience recommend sacrifice and scarcity, warfare and woe, domination and deprivation as conduits of artistic outpouring, it is nevertheless true that through such hardships can indeed come great art... and great resolve. While not the sole cause of Irish artistry, Ireland's rocky history has undoubtedly contributed to the country's rich and singular culture.

Aside from outside invaders, other privations hit the island as well, from the very ground itself, in the form of the Irish Potato Famine, the most extensive and extreme shortage of food in Europe in the 19th century. The mid-century famine led to widespread emigration of mammoth proportions, with millions of people leaving their homes due to a blight on the main food source for so many of the Irish: potatoes.

Ireland—the island—also carries the tale of two separate political entities: the Republic of Ireland *and* Northern Ireland. This book takes readers on a multifaceted tour of the Republic of Ireland (the southern and western part of the island), which, at 27,000 square miles (70,000 square kilometres), is about half the size of New York state. Ireland's population of four million people, most of whom are of primarily Celtic stock, has an ethnicity unlike that of Great Britain because the Romans never hopped the Irish Sea to conquer Ireland as they did the island of Great Britain. (The Vikings, however, did leave their genetic markers here and there in Ireland. More on that history in a bit.)

Before going any further, this is probably a good time to explain a facet of nomenclature that tends to confuse many people not from the area, namely: just what it is that constitutes Great Britain, England, and the United Kingdom... and where, in all that, Ireland figures in.

• The United Kingdom, also referred to as the United Kingdom of Great Britain and Northern Ireland, is a kind of conglomerate country consisting of England, Scotland, Wales, and Northern Ireland. The U.K.'s capital is London. (So England is not technically a country, as many erroneously believe. It is a *part* of the U.K.)

• Great Britain is the name of the island consisting of England, Scotland, and Wales. As stated earlier, it is part of the United Kingdom, which is sometimes referred to as Britain.

• The name "Ireland" is used to identify both the whole *island* of Ireland—Northern Ireland included—and the *country* or *republic* of Ireland, which is the section of the island that we will explore in this book. Therefore, Ireland the country is not part of either the United Kingdom *or* Great Britain.

The country of Ireland, though, certainly was not always its own entity, complete with its own government, economy, identity, and such. In fact, the existence of Ireland as an independent country is relatively recent.

But first things first. What we know of Ireland's history begins with the hunters and fishers who arrived in about 6000 BCE. Three thousand years later, folks with farming knowledge showed up, followed by those skilled in bronze working. Cut to 300 BCE and the arrival of the Celts, a central European people whose ironworking knowledge allowed them to dominate the earlier groups. Nearly 800 years later, at the beginning of the 5th century CE, Christianity made its way to Ireland, most famously in the form of St. Patrick (though he was not the first missionary to make his mark).

Things went fairly well on the island until a good thousand years of external control began, first in the form of marauding Vikings in the 9th and 10th centuries, and then through English rule. Readers will learn of everything from England's benign absentee landlords to the iron-fisted control of Oliver Cromwell in the 17th century, and beyond. Protestants came to dominate Ireland, and the Irish Catholics found themselves deprived of their land, their right to vote, and even the right to intermarry with the English. As time went on, the voice for home rule of Ireland grew from a whisper to a clarion call. Dissent and unrest were all around: both among the Irish against their English "overlords" as well as against other Irish who would have Ireland continue to be a jewel in England's crown, rather than a bejewelled coronet unto itself.

And although Ireland seemed on the brink of civil war when World War I broke out, that war brought an end—at least temporarily—to Ireland's internecine struggles, as there is no better way to bring two previously sparring enemies to join forces than to introduce a common foe—in this case, the Central Powers (most notably Germany, Austria-Hungary, and Ottoman Turkey). Readers will learn all about this temporary bipartisanship between both sides, and then the ensuing and momentous Easter Rebellion of 1916. Britain's bloody reprisal for that rebellion, also known as the Easter Rising, put an end to cooperative, conciliatory efforts between the two sides, sending many in Ireland a clear and pressing message: Ireland had to be its own country. This feat was begun in earnest in 1937, when the Irish Free State (established by the Anglo-Irish Treaty of 1922) wrote itself a new national constitution and dubbed itself Éire (the Gaelic name for Ireland). The final step toward independence was taken in 1949, when Ireland became a republic. The government was set up with a president who is elected by popular vote every seven years. The post is mostly ceremonial, with the real executive power residing in the office of *taoiseach* (prime minister). The legislative branch is the Oireachtas (Parliament). Decades later, as a member of the European Union (EU), Ireland adopted the EU's currency in 2002. This time, Ireland's joining forces with those beyond its borders was volitional.

Here's the thing to remember about Ireland. It is a grand place with a larger-than-life history, image, and profile. Consider Ireland and a host of iconic writers (William Butler Yeats, James Joyce, George Bernard Shaw, Oscar Wilde), visual artists (painter Francis Bacon and filmmaker Neil Jordan), musicians (U2 and Sinéad O'Connor), events (the Great Potato Famine, Bloody Sunday), a plant (the shamrock), an animal (the snake), products (beer and Waterford crystal), a form of poetry (the limerick), a specific colour (green), and even a magical creature (the leprechaun) come to mind. Then there's the recent nickname the "Celtic Tiger," based on Ireland's unprecedented economic boom in the early 1990s, a soaring economy that was later to waiver and require assistance from the EU to get back on its "paws" again.

And of course, when one considers Ireland, perhaps the very first thing that may come to mind is the lilting accent. The tone and tenor of Ireland come through loud and strong, too, even for those people who have never set foot there. Thinking or talking about Ireland may well make one want to utter an Irish expression *(Top o' the mornin' to ya!)* or to just speak in a brogue (however approximated and sometimes butchered). Ireland, its creative output and political history, as well as the Irish, all have a strong pull on the imagination, almost seeming to occupy their own geographic isle in the brain. And the pull goes far and wide, as there are more people of Irish extraction living outside the country than in it. Just in the United States alone, over 40 million Americans trace their ancestry back to Ireland, as do millions of others the world over. To these millions, Ireland is the original homeland that many yearn to go back to, and in fact, many do.

Ireland is also replete with legends. In *The Britannica Guide to Countries of the European Union: Ireland*, readers will learn the *truth* about snakes and the Emerald Isle. And speaking of snakes and the man credited with banishing them—St. Patrick—here is a spoiler alert: he was not even born in Ireland. Nor, it seems, were any snakes. (Apparently, the island never had any snakes to banish.) Details about St. Patrick's storied life await within. What is more, although green is the colour we all associate with him, the day named for him, and the country itself, blue was actually the colour traditionally and originally associated with the great saint.

That original blue notwithstanding, though, green plus Ireland conjures images of rolling countryside, and there is plenty of that on Éire, but the truth of the matter is that more than one-quarter of the country's population lives in Dublin, the country's sophisticated, entertaining, and affluent capital. Cork is Ireland's second largest city, one known for its cathedrals and ports.

Ireland is now part of the European Union, and it is as urbane and sophisticated as any of its fellow member states. Yet there is something in the Irish heart that yearns for the past (as hard as it was) and country life (as hard as it can be) summed up in these lines from the great poet of Ireland, the aforementioned W.B. Yeats:

> An acre of stony ground,
> Where the symbolic rose can
> break in flower,
> Old ragged elms, old thorns
> innumerable,
> The sound of the rain or sound
> Of every wind that blows;
> The stilted water-hen
> Crossing stream again
> Scared by the splashing of a
> dozen cows.

And there's also the salty side of Ireland, best wrapped up in the poetic form of poetry known as the limerick, its origin generally ascribed to the eponymous Irish city:

> The limerick packs laughs
> anatomical
> Into space that is quite
> economical.
> But the good ones I've seen
> So seldom are clean
> And the clean ones so seldom
> are comical.

—Anonymous

Here is Ireland, a detailed account of a country of great history, tradition, sophistication, culture, cows, and comedy. Fáilte!*

*Welcome, in Irish, pronounced FAHLT-shuh.

CHAPTER 1

LAND

The magnificent scenery of Ireland's Atlantic coastline faces a 2,000-mile-wide (3,200 km) expanse of ocean, and its geographic isolation has helped it to develop a rich heritage of culture and tradition that was linked initially to the Gaelic language. Washed by abundant rain, the country's pervasive grasslands create a green-hued landscape that is responsible for the popular sobriquet Emerald Isle. Ireland is also renowned for its wealth of folklore, from tales of tiny leprechauns with hidden pots of gold to that of the patron saint, Patrick, with his legendary ridding the island of snakes and his reputed use of the three-leaved shamrock as a symbol for the Christian Trinity. But while many may think of Ireland as an enchanted land, the republic has been beset with perennial concerns—emigration, cultural and political identity, and relations with Northern Ireland (comprising the 6 of Ireland's 32 counties within the province of Ulster that remain part of the United Kingdom). At the beginning of the 21st century, Ireland's long-standing economic problems were abating, owing to its diverse, export-driven economy; however, calamity struck again in 2008 when a new financial and economic crisis befell the country.

The Republic of Ireland occupies the greater part of an island lying to the west of Great Britain, from which it is separated—at distances ranging from 11 to 120 miles (18 to 193 km)—by the North Channel, the Irish Sea, and St. George's Channel. Located in the temperate zone between latitudes 51°30 and 55°30 N and longitudes 6°00 and 10°30 W

Political map of Ireland.

—as far north as Labrador or British Columbia in Canada and as far west as the West African state of Liberia—it constitutes the westernmost outpost of the Atlantic fringe of the Eurasian landmass. Ireland, which, like Great Britain, once formed part of this landmass, lies on the European continental shelf, surrounded by seas that are generally less than 650 feet (200 metres) deep. The greatest distance from north to south in the island is 302 miles (486 km), and from east to west it is 171 miles (275 km).

The flag of Ireland.

RELIEF

The territory of the republic consists of a broad and undulating central plain underlain by limestone. This plain is ringed almost completely by coastal highlands, which vary considerably in geologic structure. The flatness of the central lowland—which lies for the most part between 200 and 400 feet (60 and 120 m) above sea level—is relieved in many places by low hills between 600 and 1,000 feet (180 to 300 m) in elevation. With many lakes, large bog areas, and low ridges, the lowland is very scenic. The principal mountain ranges are the Blue Stack Mountains in the north, the Wicklow Mountains in the east (topped by Lugnaquillia, at 3,039 feet [926 m]), the Knockmealdown and Comeragh mountains in the south, the Macgillycuddy's Reeks in the southwest, and the Twelve Pins in the west. Carrantuohill, at 3,414 feet (1,041 m) in the Macgillycuddy's

Reeks, is the highest point in the republic. In the west and southwest the wild and beautiful coast is heavily indented where the mountains of Donegal, Mayo, Galway, and Kerry thrust out into the Atlantic, separated by deep, wide-mouthed bays, some of which—Bantry Bay and Dingle Bay, for example—are, in fact, drowned river valleys. By contrast, the east coast is little indented, but most of the country's trade passes through its ports because of their proximity to British and Continental markets.

The coastal mountain fringe illustrates the country's complex geologic history. In the west and northwest as well as in the east, the mountains are composed mainly of granite. Old Red Sandstone predominates in the south, where the parallel folded mountain ridges trend east-west, separated by limestone river valleys. Ireland experienced at least two general glaciations—one covering most of the country and the other extending as far south as a line linking

Limerick, Cashel, and Dublin—and the characteristic diversity of Irish scenery owes much to this glacial influence. The large areas of peat bog to be found throughout the country are a notable feature of the landscape.

DRAINAGE

The rivers that rise on the seaward side of the coastal mountain fringe are naturally short and rapid. The inland streams, however, flow slowly, often through marshes and lakes, and enter the sea—usually by way of waterfalls and rapids—long distances from their sources. The famed River Shannon, for example, rises in the plateau country near Sligo Bay and flows sluggishly south-southwestward for some 160 miles (260 km), reaching tidewater level at Limerick and draining a wide area of the central lowland on its way. Other major inland rivers—some of them renowned for their salmon fisheries—are the Slaney, Liffey, and Boyne in the east; the Nore, Barrow, and Suir in the southeast; the Blackwater, Lee, and Bandon in the south; and the Clare and the Moy in the west. Because of the porosity of the underlying Carboniferous limestones, an underground drainage system has developed, feeding the interlacing surface network of rivers and lakes. The government has implemented major arterial drainage projects, preventing flooding—and making more land available for

RIVER SHANNON

The longest river in Ireland, the River Shannon rises in northwestern County Cavan and flows for about 161 miles (259 km) in a southerly direction to enter the Atlantic Ocean via a 70-mile (113-km) estuary below Limerick city. It drains an area of 6,060 square miles (15,695 square km). As the main river draining the central lowland of Ireland, it is surrounded by marshes and bogs for much of its course and widens at various points into lakes, many with islands.

The source of the Shannon is generally considered to be the pools at the foot of Tiltinbane Mountain. After a few miles it enters Lough Allen and then flows south through a wide belt of marshes and water meadows. It is crossed by a bridge at Leitrim and at Carrick-on-Shannon, above which it is joined by the Boyle from the west. From north of Carrick south to Roosky, it flows through a landscape dominated by hills of glacial drift (drumlins) interspersed with bogs and marshes. Near Termonbarry, at Richmond Harbour, the river is joined by the Royal Canal; and at Lanesborough it enters Lough Ree.

The bridge at Athlone is 15 miles (24 km) from the next at Shannonbridge, where the Suck, the largest tributary, joins the main river. At Shannon Harbour the river is joined by the Grand Canal. About 15 miles south it reaches Lough Derg at Portumna, and its waters feed the Ardnacrusha hydroelectric power station, using the fall of 109 feet (33 metres) from lake to sea level. A fish ladder at the outlet of Lough Derg allows salmon to pass upriver to spawn. From Limerick the river enters its long estuary, in which shipping has dwindled since the 19th century and in which some of the large reclaimed areas have been used for Shannon International Airport, located near the estuary of the River Fergus in County Clare.

In the early part of the 19th century, the Shannon was a vital link in the waterways of Ireland. From 1755 the Grand Canal was constructed across the central lowland, reaching the Shannon in 1804. From 1789 to 1817 the Royal Canal was constructed from the north side of Dublin through Mullingar to the Shannon, but it was not so successful as was the Grand Canal, and it was sold to a railway company in 1846. At that time steamers used the Shannon between Killaloe and Richmond

The River Shannon at Limerick, County Limerick. Tourism Ireland

Harbour, and horsedrawn boats went on the canal from Killaloe to Limerick. There were passenger services along the canals from 1780 onward, but they ceased in the 1850s because of rail competition. The Shannon steamboats survived as a tourist attraction until World War I. Many parts of the river are used for pleasure craft.

cultivation—by improving the flow of water in the rivers and thereby lowering the levels of lakes. There are also state-aided farm drainage schemes designed to bring wasteland and marginal land into production.

SOILS

Most Irish soils originate from drift, the ice-scoured waste formerly frozen to the base of the advancing glaciers. Some older rocks in the country's geologic formation—quartzites, certain granites, and shales—weather into infertile and unproductive soils. In many places, however, these have been overlaid by patches of the ice-borne drift, mostly limestone-bearing, which are farmed with considerable success. The bare limestone regions remaining in western areas show how much glacial drift cover has meant to the Irish agricultural economy.

CLIMATE

Ireland's climate is classified as western maritime. The predominant influence is the Atlantic Ocean, which is no more than 70 miles (112 km) from any inland location. The mild southwesterly winds and warm waters of the North Atlantic Current contribute to the moderate quality of the climate. Temperature is almost

Cows on the verdant rural fields of County Cork. John W Banagan/Lonely Planet Images/ Getty Images

uniform over the entire island. Average air temperatures lie mainly between limits of 39 and 45 °F (4 and 7 °C) in January and February, the coldest months of the year. In July and August, the warmest months, temperatures usually range between 57 and 61 °F (14 and 16 °C), although occasionally considerably higher readings are recorded. The sunniest months are May and June, when there is sunshine for an average duration of 5.5 and 6.5 hours a day, respectively, over most of the country and the ancient patchwork of fields and settlements making up the landscape glows under a clear, vital light. Average annual precipitation varies from about 30 inches (760 millimetres) in the east to more than 100 inches (2,533 mm) in the western areas exposed to the darkening clouds that often come sweeping in from the Atlantic. The precipitation, combined with the equable climate, is particularly beneficial to the grasslands, which are the mainstay of the country's large livestock population. Snow is infrequent except in the mountains, and prolonged or severe snowstorms are rare.

PLANT AND ANIMAL LIFE

Ireland was almost completely covered by glaciers during the Ice Age, and its plant and animal life are thus mainly—but not entirely—the result of the subsequent migration of species from other areas. As long as there was a land connection between Ireland and what was to become the rest of the British Isles, most species arrived overland from northern Europe. Irish plant and animal life nevertheless possess certain unique features owing partly to climatic conditions and partly

NORTH ATLANTIC CURRENT

The North Atlantic Current (which is also called the North Atlantic Drift) is part of a clockwise-setting ocean-current system in the North Atlantic Ocean that extends from southeast of the Grand Bank, off Newfoundland, Canada, to the Norwegian Sea, off northwestern Europe. It constitutes the northeastward extension of the Gulf Stream; the latter issues from the Gulf of Mexico and gradually emerges as the North Atlantic Current in mid-ocean. It is composed of several broad currents with speeds of about 0.2 knots, as compared with the Gulf Stream's rather concentrated flow at 1 to 6 knots.

Characterized by warm temperature and high salinity, the North Atlantic Current is sometimes concealed at the surface by shallow and variable wind-drift movements. The current often mixes with northern cold polar water to produce excellent fishing grounds near islands and along the coast of northwestern Europe. The combination of the warm current and prevailing westerly winds helps maintain a mild climate in northwestern Europe. Major branches of the current include the Irminger, Norway, and Canary currents.

to the fact that Ireland became separated from Britain by the Irish Sea sometime before Britain itself became separated from the European continent.

Apart from flora that came from northern Europe, several plants common in Ireland are believed to have reached the country from the Mediterranean, along a subsequently drowned coastal route, and others appear to have arrived from North America, probably by way of Greenland and Iceland. The western highlands are home to such hardy species as St. Dabeoc's heath, Irish spurge, *Eriocaulon aquaticum* (a pipewort with North American affinities), and the Irish orchid (a species of Mediterranean origin). Scattered over the island are sundew, foxglove, bell heather, sheep's bit, bog asphodel, and yellow fleabane—yet it is Ireland's extensive and verdant grasslands that leave the most lasting impression. Prior to the 17th century the Irish midlands had great forests of broad-leaved trees, but by the end of the 19th century the once large forests had been reduced to about 1 percent of the total land area. Now the island is mainly devoid of broad-leaved woodlands, and government-sponsored reforestation programs have chiefly favoured fast-growing sitka spruce.

Common English animals such as the weasel and the mole do not exist in Ireland, which also has no snakes. Tradition ascribes the absence of snakes to banishment at the hands of St. Patrick; in fact, before their introduction as pets and in zoos in the 20th century, snakes had not lived on the island for the thousands of years since the Ice Age. In addition, there are only two kinds of mice—as opposed to four in Britain—and the only reptile found in Ireland is a species of lizard. Endemic mammals include the Irish stoat and Irish hare. Deer have increased in number since the mid-19th century, but the giant Irish elk has long been extinct. Ireland abounds in birdlife, notably waterfowl. Numerous species that breed in Iceland and Greenland in the summer spend winter in Ireland, and many more migratory species stop there in the spring and fall.

CHAPTER 2

PEOPLE

Although Ireland was invaded and colonized within historical times by Celts, Norsemen, Normans, English, and Scots, there are no corresponding ethnic distinctions. Ireland has always been known as a welcoming place, and diversity is not a phenomenon new to the country.

Women in the centre of Dublin, smartphones at the ready.
Hope Lourie Killcoyne

ETHNIC GROUPS, LANGUAGE, AND RELIGION

Ethnic and racial minorities make up about 12 percent of the population of Ireland—a proportion that doubled in the first decade of the 21st century. Immigration from Europe, Africa, and Asia has been significant since the last two decades of the 20th century. The key factors in increased immigration have been the more-open labour market provided by the European Union and the globalized nature of the contemporary Irish economy, both which have attracted a wave of new residents. Today Poles constitute the largest minority population in Ireland. Although they are small in number, the nomadic Travellers ("Tinkers") are an indigenous ethnic minority group—defined by their shared customs, traditions, and language—who have lived in Ireland for centuries.

The constitution provides that Irish be the first official language and English the second. All official documents are published in both Irish and English. The modern Irish language, which is very similar to Scottish Gaelic, was widely spoken up to the time of the Irish Potato Famine of the 1840s (*see* chapter 7) and the subsequent emigrations. The use of Irish continued to decline even after 1922, when the language was introduced into schools; despite its decline, Irish never ceased to exert a strong influence on Irish consciousness. Although its use as a vernacular has decreased and is concentrated in several small Gaeltacht (i.e., Irish-speaking) areas, Irish is more widely read, spoken, and understood today than it had been during most of the 20th century. English is universally spoken. Compulsory Gaelic in Irish schools has come under some criticism from the business sector, which would prefer to see students develop more-diverse language skills, as well as from some other quarters.

The Celtic religion had a major influence on Ireland long before the adoption

IRISH LANGUAGE

The Irish language (referred to in Irish as Gaeilge; also called Erse) is a member of the Goidelic group of Celtic languages. As one of the national languages of the Republic of Ireland, Irish is taught in the public schools and is required for certain civil-service posts.

Grammatically, Irish still has a case system, like Latin or German, with four cases to show differing functions of nouns and pronouns in a sentence. In phonology it exhibits initial sandhi, in which the first consonant of a word is modified according to the prehistoric final sound of the previous word in the phrase (e.g., *an tobar* "the well," *mo thobar* "my well").

Records in the Irish language date back to the ogham inscriptions, written in sets of strokes or notches, of the 5th century; the Latin alphabet began to be used shortly thereafter. Irish literature dates from the 8th century.

of Christianity in the 5th century. Its precise rituals and beliefs remain somewhat obscure, but the names of hundreds of Celtic gods have survived, and elements of the religion—particularly the cults of Mary (an echo of Danu, the Earth Mother goddess whom the Celts worshiped) and St. Brigit (one of Ireland's patron saints) and several seasonal festivals—carried into the Christian period.

Since the conversion to Christianity, Roman Catholicism, with its ecclesiastical seat at Armagh in Northern Ireland, has been the island's principal religion.

St. Patrick's Cathedral, Dublin. © Digital Vision/Getty Images

After the Reformation, Catholicism became closely associated with Irish nationalism and resistance to British rule. However, church support for nationalism—both then and now—has been ambivalent. After the devastating Irish Potato Famine in the 1840s, there was a remarkable surge in devotional support of the Catholic Church, and over the next century the number of Irish priests, nuns, and missionaries grew dramatically.

Today, more than four-fifths of the republic's population is Roman Catholic, with small numbers of other religious groups (including Church of Ireland Anglicans, Presbyterians, Methodists, Muslims, and Jews). There is no officially established church in Ireland, and the freedoms of conscience and religion are constitutionally guaranteed. Since the last decades of the 20th century, Ireland has seen a significant decline in the number of regular churchgoers. That decline corresponded with the heyday of the so-called Celtic Tiger economy—when, during the 1990s in particular, robust economic growth made the country significantly wealthier—and also with the revelations of child abuse by Catholic clergy that came to light in the first decade of the 21st century. The Roman Catholic Church nevertheless continues to play a prominent role in the country, including maintaining responsibility for most schools and many hospitals.

SETTLEMENT PATTERNS

The country's size contributes to its historically homogeneous population and helps explain the distinctive character of "Irishness" that emerged over time. This historical homogeneity also has worked against the development of significant regional or local divisions. One regional distinction is that between the part of the country east of the River Shannon—with its industrial employment, fertile farmlands, economic growth, and rising standard of living—and the poorer areas of the west—particularly west Donegal, Leitrim, west Mayo, west Galway, Clare, west Cork, and south Kerry—where incomes were traditionally low (though they are now supplemented by industrial development and tourism) and the fertility of the land was in many cases insufficient to provide an acceptable standard of living for the people. These western areas include the districts known collectively as the Gaeltacht, in which the Irish language and the traditional national culture are best preserved. Emigration abroad or to cities within Ireland has always been among the chief threats to the survival of this cultural heritage.

DEMOGRAPHIC TRENDS

The republic's marriage, birth, and death rates are comparable to those of nearby countries. For example, life expectancy is about 75 years for men and 80 for women. Historically, the rate of emigration—which had been greatly in excess of the next highest rate in Europe—depleted Ireland's population. As a result of emigration, hundreds of thousands of Irish-born

COUNTY CLARE

County Clare (Irish: An Clár) is located in the province of Munster in western Ireland. It comprises three parts. In the east are peat- and bog-covered hills rising to 1,750 feet (533 m), including the Slieve Bernagh, Slieve Aughty, and Cratloe hills, which are penetrated by wide valleys. Lowland central Clare has drained and embanked areas of former salt marsh along the Shannon and Fergus estuaries, and around Galway Bay the limestone country merges into the central Irish lowland. Surface drainage is restricted by the limestone: rivers often disappear underground, and in many turloughs, or limestone hollows, water may lie indefinitely.

West Clare comprises plateaus and lowlands. The Burren is a distinctive region of almost horizontal limestone slabs and little vegetation; along the coast is a limestone pavement area. The vegetation of the Burren comprises an unusual mixture of north and south European and alpine plants. The Burren plateau has a stony, desertlike appearance and is edged in places by steep, terraced rock faces. A flagstone occurs in some of the cliff faces, including the cliffs of Moher (600 feet [180 m]) along the Atlantic.

Beach at Kilkee, County Clare. Chris Hill/Tourism Ireland

Bunratty Castle on the River Shannon, County Clare. G.F. Allen-Bruce Coleman Inc./EB Inc.

Clare has mild winters and rainy summers; much of the county's land is devoted to crops and pastures, and the main resources are cattle and sheep. Farms average 40–50 acres (16–20 hectares), and the chief crops are oats and potatoes. Most settlements are small trading centres, and Lisdoonvarna is a spa town. Ardnacrusha, on the Shannon, has a large hydroelectric-power station. Shannon International Airport is on reclaimed land 12 miles (19 km) southeast of Ennis. During the latter decades of the 20th century, the county experienced significant industrial development.

Clare abounds in evidence of prehistoric settlement, particularly from the Neolithic Period (New Stone Age) and the Bronze Age, including many megaliths and some 2,000 fortified enclosures. There are many early Christian sites with round towers and medieval castles—notably Bunratty Castle. Clare was part of Thomond, or North Munster, of which the O'Briens remained lords until the 16th century, despite the Anglo-Norman colonization in the 12th century. Clare was made a shire in the reign of Elizabeth I. In 1828 Daniel O'Connell won the election in Clare that led to the emancipation of Catholics in Ireland. The largest towns are Ennis, the county town (seat), and Kilrush. The seat of the Roman Catholic diocese is in Ennis, and the Church of Ireland cathedral is in Killaloe.

people now live outside their native land, and millions of citizens of other countries are of Irish extraction. However, in the 1990s immigration to Ireland outpaced emigration from the country. New immigrants included a large number of Irish Americans moving back to the country.

This trend reversed dramatically beginning in 2008, when the vaunted Celtic Tiger economy collapsed and a new wave of Irish emigration started. Unlike previous waves, this new set of departing Irish was made up largely of high-skilled labourers and the highly educated.

CHAPTER 3

ECONOMY

Ireland has a mixed economy. The constitution provides that the state shall favour private initiative in industry and commerce, but the state may provide essential services and promote development projects in the absence of private initiatives. Thus, state-sponsored ("semi-state") bodies operate the country's rail and road transport, some of its television and radio stations, its electricity generation and distribution system, and its peat industry. State companies are also active in the fields of air transport and health insurance. The advent of a single European market in the 1990s encouraged many of these enterprises to privatize and become more competitive.

Ireland's high-technology sector—made attractive by a very low 12.5 percent corporate tax rate—spurred economic growth during the 1990s and helped reduce unemployment to historically low levels. The economic boom, during which the country's growth was more than double that of most other EU countries, gave rise to the country's being labelled the "Celtic Tiger." By 2001, however, the benefits of new jobs created by foreign direct investment via multinational corporations began to slow. Still focused on high growth, Ireland's political leadership and its banking sector turned to the mortgage and construction industries to maintain growth. By 2008 it had become clear that much of the growth in banking and construction was a bubble without capital to back it. Collapse soon followed, and Ireland went into deep economic recession for several years. A bailout of the Irish financial system by the European Union (EU) and the International Monetary Fund (IMF) in 2010 was accompanied by requirements for deep austerity cuts that further dampened prospects for the domestic Irish economy. Ireland had benefited in the 1990s and early 2000s from a combination of low tax rates and responsive social programs; however, both contributed to the significant budget challenges that came as result of the 2008 financial collapse.

When Ireland joined the European Economic Community (EEC; now the EU) in 1973, more than half of its trade was with the United Kingdom. Although this proportion has declined, economic relations between the two countries have remained close.

AGRICULTURE, FORESTRY, AND FISHING

Once the mainstay of the national economy, agriculture continues to be important. Most of Ireland's agricultural land is used as pasture or for growing hay. The climate fosters abundant vegetable and other plant growth and is particularly beneficial to the rich grasslands that enable grazing stock to be kept on pasture almost year-round. Most farms are family farms; only a small percentage of those employed in agriculture work as hired labour. Mixed farming is the general pattern, with the production of beef cattle tending to predominate in the midlands and dairy farming in the south. Cereal growing is an important activity in the east and southeast. Sheep raising is widespread on the rugged hills and mountain slopes throughout the country.

Most of the gross agricultural output consists of livestock and livestock products, with beef as the biggest single item, followed by milk and pigs. Other important products are cereals (particularly barley and wheat), poultry and eggs, sheep and wool, and root crops, including sugar beets and potatoes. Indeed, enough beets are grown to meet the country's sugar requirements. Since the 1980s farmhouse cheese production has flourished, and other specialized food production (e.g., organically produced vegetables) has increased. The bloodstock (Thoroughbred) industry is a thriving economic sector and has won worldwide fame for the Irish racehorse.

Adverse conditions in export markets following World War II handicapped the expansion of Irish agriculture, and the subsequent growth of agricultural output was slower than that in the industrial and service sectors. This situation was ameliorated with the republic's entrance into the EEC in 1973. After a two-decade decline, farm incomes began to rise in the 1990s.

When Ireland was established as an independent country in 1922, woodland represented less than 1 percent of the total land area, but state replanting since World War II has increased almost eightfold the acreage under forests and woodlands. Private afforestation efforts also increased in the late 20th century. A state-owned company was established in

1988 to manage the republic's commercial forestry. Sea fishing and aquaculture resources have been developed since the mid-20th century, but, because the most extensive fishing grounds in the EU are off Ireland's shores, international competition is intense.

RESOURCES AND POWER

Ireland is not rich in mineral resources. Discoveries of silver, lead, zinc, and gypsum have been successfully developed, but the country's dependence on imports for its energy requirements is high. In the early 1980s offshore natural gas wells began production in the Celtic Sea south of County Cork. The offshore reserves were limited, however, and a pipeline from Britain was built in the 1990s to provide replacement supplies.

For centuries hand-cut peat, or turf, was the rural population's principal domestic fuel. Virtually all rural households are now connected to the national electricity network, which relies partly on hydroelectric plants and on small and medium-sized peat-burning thermal power stations. Although peat production was mechanized and industrialized in the 20th century, peat was largely supplanted by natural gas and by coal and oil imports.

There remains today some potential for natural gas exploration off the Irish territorial sea, but the major areas for innovation come from the potential for wind and wave energy development. In July 2009 the country set a national record for energy output from wind, generating 999 megawatts—enough to power over 650,000 houses, or about one-third of Ireland's daily energy needs.

MANUFACTURING

Until World War II and for some years after it, official manufacturing policy was nationalistic and protectionist. High tariffs and quotas protected young industries, which provided badly needed employment and helped to supply the home market but which had little or no export potential. From the mid-1950s onward the protectionist policies were progressively reversed. The principal basis of the government's Programmes for Economic Expansion was an industrial development policy designed—by means of tax concessions, financial grants, and other incentives—first, to encourage existing industries to increase their competitive strength and seek markets abroad and, second, to attract new manufacturing enterprises, whether foreign or Irish-owned, to the republic.

The policy achieved a large measure of success. By the late 20th century a larger proportion of the labour force was employed in manufacturing than in agriculture, and the industrial sector accounted for most of Ireland's total export earnings. A competitive economy became all the more desirable in view of the governmental obligation to demobilize protective tariffs in accordance with the single European market and the World

Trade Organization. Since the 1970s computer and software equipment and international financial and other services have become important economic sectors.

FINANCE

The Irish pound (or punt) was linked to the British pound sterling until 1979, when the republic joined the European Monetary System. Today, the euro, the EU's single currency, is the country's official currency. The Central Bank of Ireland, established in 1942, is the national monetary authority. Its responsibilities include licensing and overseeing the country's financial institutions and supervising the Irish Stock Exchange. The bank does

EURO

The euro is the monetary unit and currency of the European Union and is, as such, the currency of Ireland. It was introduced as a noncash monetary unit in 1999, and currency notes and coins appeared in participating countries on January 1, 2002. After February 28, 2002, the euro became the sole currency of member states, and their national currencies ceased to be legal tender. The euro is represented by the symbol €.

The euro's origins lay in the Maastricht Treaty (1991), an agreement among the then 12 member countries of the European Community (now the European Union)—United Kingdom, France, Germany, Italy, Ireland, Belgium, Denmark, the Netherlands, Spain, Portugal, Greece, and Luxembourg—that included the creation of an economic and monetary union (EMU). The treaty called for a common unit of exchange, the euro, and set strict criteria for conversion to the euro and participation in the EMU. These requirements included annual budget deficits not exceeding 3 percent of gross domestic product (GDP), public debt under 60 percent of GDP, exchange rate stability, inflation rates within 1.5 percent of the three lowest inflation rates in the EU, and long-term inflation rates within 2 percent. Although several states had public debt ratios exceeding 60 percent, the European Commission (the executive branch of the EU) recommended their entry into the EMU, citing the significant steps each country had taken to reduce its debt ratio.

Supporters of the euro argued that a single European currency would boost trade by eliminating foreign exchange fluctuations and reducing prices. Although there were concerns regarding a single currency, including worries about counterfeiting and loss of national sovereignty and national identity, 11 countries (Austria, Belgium, Finland, France, Germany, Ireland, Italy, Luxembourg, the Netherlands, Portugal, and Spain) formally joined the EMU in 1998. Britain and Sweden delayed joining, though some businesses in Britain decided to accept payment in euros. Voters in Denmark narrowly rejected the euro in a September 2000 referendum. Greece initially failed to meet the economic requirements but was admitted in January 2001 after overhauling its economy. In 2007 Slovenia became the first former communist country to adopt the euro. Having demonstrated fiscal stability since joining the EU in 2004, both Malta and the Greek Cypriot sector of Cyprus adopted the euro in 2008. Other countries that adopted the currency include Slovakia (2009) and Estonia (2011). (The euro is also the official currency in several areas outside the EU, including Andorra, Montenegro, and San Marino.) The participating countries are known as the euro area, euroland, or the euro zone. In 1998 the European Central Bank (ECB) was established to manage the new currency. Based in Frankfurt, Germany, the ECB is an independent and neutral body headed by an appointed president who is approved by all member countries to serve an eight-year term.

The euro was launched on January 1, 1999, replacing the precursor ecu at a 1:1 value. Until the circulation of currency notes and coins in 2002, the euro was used only by financial markets and certain businesses. At

Map indicating which members of the European Union use the euro as their national currency. The Republic of Cyprus (not shown) has also adopted the euro.

its launch, many experts predicted that the euro could eventually rival the dollar as an international currency.

Unlike most of the national currencies that they replaced, euro banknotes do not display famous national figures. The seven colourful bills, designed by the Austrian artist Robert Kalina and ranging in denomination from €5 to €500, symbolize the unity of Europe and feature a map of Europe, the EU's flag, and arches, bridges, gateways, and windows. The eight euro coins range in denominations from one cent to two euros. The coins feature one side with a common design; the reverse sides' designs differ in each of the individual participating countries.

not transact business with the public, but it exerts a considerable influence on the volume of bank credit through the "advice" it gives to the clearing (or, to use the Irish term, the associated) banks. The Irish Stock Exchange, located in central Dublin, is one of the oldest in the world, having traded continuously since 1793.

The collapse of the Irish economy in late 2008 created economic chaos in the country. Initially, the government believed that failing banks would attract investment after it pledged to guarantee all deposits in those banks. Instead, the government's promise left the Irish people liable for losses of staggering proportions for such a small country. Ireland fought to manage its situation through November 2010, but it ultimately accepted a bailout of more than $100 billion from the EU, the IMF, and countries offering bilateral aid. The terms of the bailout set by the EU and the IMF were very stringent.

TRADE

The United Kingdom remains Ireland's chief trading partner. Other major partners include the other countries of the EU (notably Germany, France, and the Netherlands), the United States, Japan, and Singapore. A wide range of manufactured products is exported, including electrical machinery and apparatus, processed foods, chemical products, clothing and textiles, and beverages. Ireland is among the world's leading exporters of computer software. The principal imports include machinery and transport equipment, chemicals, petroleum and petroleum products, food products, and textiles.

SERVICES

Tourism plays a very important role in the Irish economy. Its value has increased considerably since the 1950s, when the Irish Tourist Board (Bord Fáilte Éireann)

The front entrance to the Guinness Storehouse. Part museum, part bar, it is one of Dublin's most popular tourist attractions. Construction on the storehouse began in 1902 for use as a fermentation house. Hope Lourie Killcoyne

was established and began encouraging new hotel construction, the development of resort areas, the extension of sporting facilities, and an increase of tourist amenities. The organization's successor, Fáilte Ireland, also developed joint ventures with the Northern Ireland Tourist Board. The vast majority of foreign tourists come from the United Kingdom, the United States, and elsewhere in Europe, but groups from the Middle East and China are increasingly seen at the major tourist attractions around the country.

LABOUR AND TAXATION

Almost all Irish trade unions are affiliated with the Irish Congress of Trade Unions (ICTU). The level of unionization in Ireland is fairly high, encompassing roughly one-third of the total workforce. There are also several employers' unions (industrial organizations), organized on both a craft and a regional basis. The employers' central negotiating organization is the Irish Business and Employers Confederation. Wages and employment conditions are normally subject to free collective bargaining, though industrial disputes may be referred to the Labour Relations Commission (created in 1990) or to the Labour Court (set up in 1946). In the late 1980s, when the economy faced serious problems, the government, employers, and unions agreed on a recovery program. Similar partnerships were adopted in the 1990s and have become a feature of the country's economic and social management.

The social compact between unions and government survived the crash of the Irish economy in 2008 via a negotiation known as the Croke Park Agreement, which largely saved union jobs in favour of agreed-to wage and benefit cuts. Public-sector unions in Ireland are powerful, but, because of the social compact with the government, major public demonstrations and work stoppages were avoided even in the face of increasing austerity measures.

Compared with the rest of the industrialized world, Ireland has relatively low rates of corporate and individual income taxes. In contrast, the country's value-added (consumption) tax (VAT) is fairly high and is charged on most goods and services.

TRANSPORTATION

As a result of its scattered rural population, Ireland has a large road system. Most local roads are well-surfaced, and continuous progress has been made toward bringing the arterial roads up to the best modern standards. Ireland has benefited from funds received from the EU to improve and develop its transportation infrastructure. Still, the overall growth of large urban areas such as Dublin has outpaced much of the road infrastructure, which was planned before much of the economic expansion of the 1990s and early 2000s. Commuting by car and public parking in Ireland's large cities have become increasingly problematic.

The Irish Transport System (Córas Iompair Éireann) has financial control over three autonomous operating companies—Irish Rail (Iarnród Éireann), Dublin Bus (Bus Átha Cliath), and Irish Bus (Bus Éireann). An electrified commuter rail system, the Dublin Area Rapid Transport, opened in Dublin in 1984. There are rail services between the principal cities and towns (including a link with Northern Ireland Railways via Belfast), but many branch lines have become uneconomic and have been replaced by road services for passengers and goods. Dublin also has introduced Luas, a light rail tram system which serves vital parts of the city centre.

There is no longer any significant commercial traffic on Irish canals. The two major canals in the country—the Royal Canal, which joins the River Shannon with the Irish Sea via Mullingar and Dublin, and the Grand Canal, which also runs from the Shannon to the Irish Sea but with a branch to the River Barrow—are maintained for use by pleasure craft. The successful restoration in the 1990s of the Shannon-Erne waterway in the northwest led to the redevelopment of other waterways in the republic and in Northern Ireland.

Smaller ports are important to the local business communities, but most of the country's seaborne trade tends to be conducted through the principal east- and south-coast ports, particularly Dublin, Waterford, and Cork. The ports in Limerick and Galway serve western Ireland. Dún Laoghaire, Dublin, Rosslare, and Cork are served by modern cross-channel passenger, motor-vehicle, and freight services to Britain, and there also are some ferry services to the Continent. The trend toward larger vessels and the shipment of goods in containers has adversely affected the smaller Irish ports, as well as the smaller privately owned shipping companies. Only a fraction of the country's foreign trade is carried by the small Irish merchant fleet.

International airports are located at Dublin, Shannon, and Cork, and there are several regional airports. Dublin Airport Authority, a public limited-liability company, has responsibility for the operation, management, and development of the three major international airports. Shannon was the world's first duty-free airport; a state-sponsored company offers substantial tax breaks and other advantages to manufacturing and warehousing concerns proposing to establish plants within the entire Shannon (midwestern) region. Aer Lingus, founded as the national airline in 1936, was privatized in the 21st century. Ireland also has seen growth in private air travel, most notably that of Ryanair, which began operation in 1985 and has served as a model for lower-fare European air travel.

TELECOMMUNICATIONS

Until the deregulation of the telecommunications sector in Ireland in 1998, the market was dominated by the

AER LINGUS

The Irish international air carrier Aer Lingus originated as the national airline of Ireland and resulted from the combination of two government-owned companies: (1) Aer Lingus Teoranta, incorporated in 1936 and operating air services within Ireland and between Ireland and Britain and continental Europe, and (2) Aerlinte Eireann Teoranta, incorporated in 1947 and operating air services between Ireland and the United States and Canada.

The airline's first route, inaugurated on May 27, 1936, extended from Dublin to Bristol and, in the same year, was extended to London. Other flights prior to World War II were routed to Liverpool and the Isle of Man. After the war, service was inaugurated to Paris and Amsterdam and eventually expanded to other European cities. The first transatlantic routes, from Dublin through Shannon International Airport to New York and Boston, were inaugurated in 1958; flights to Chicago and Montreal began in 1966. The Irish government privatized the airline in 2006.

Aer Lingus Airbus A320-200. Adrian Pingstone

state-owned Telecom Éireann (now Éircom), which subsequently formed Telecom Ireland, a subsidiary that focused its efforts on attracting foreign investment. Since deregulation, major telecommunications companies such as Norway's Telenor, British Telecom, and AT&T have operated extensively throughout Ireland. In 1997 the Irish government established the Office of the Director of Telecommunications Regulation, which was succeeded in 2002 by the Commission for Communications Regulation. It is responsible for ensuring that the liberalized telecommunications sector works in accordance with EU and Irish law. Internet use grew rapidly during the late 1990s. Whereas in 1997 less than 5 percent of the population had Internet access, less than five years later the number had grown to about one-third of the total population. Ireland was slow in getting high-speed Internet to locations around the country, but it now has achieved standards generally accepted for wireless access in Europe.

CHAPTER 4

GOVERNMENT AND SOCIETY

The Irish republic is a parliamentary democracy. Its constitution was promulgated in 1937 and can be amended through a referendum. The country's head of state, the president (*uachtarán*), is elected directly by the public for a term of seven years and is eligible for reelection for a second term. The president normally acts on the advice of the government but also consults an advisory Council of State in the exercise of certain functions. The president signs and promulgates bills passed by the Oireachtas (Parliament) and, when so advised by the prime minister (*taoiseach*), summons and dissolves the Oireachtas. The president may, however, refuse to dissolve the Oireachtas on the advice of a prime minister who has ceased to command a majority in the Dáil Éireann (House of Representatives). The president is the guardian of the constitution and may, in certain circumstances, submit a bill passed by the Oireachtas to the people in a referendum or refer it to the Supreme Court to decide on its constitutionality.

There are two houses of the Oireachtas—the Dáil and the Seanad Éireann (Senate). Chief legislative power is centred in the 166-member Dáil. The Seanad may delay bills passed by the Dáil, or it may suggest changes in them, but it cannot indefinitely block their passage into law.

Executive power is vested in the prime minister, who heads the cabinet and presides over its meetings. The prime minister, the deputy prime minister (*tánaiste*), and the minister for finance must be members of the Dáil. The other government ministers must be members of either house, but no more than two may be senators.

LOCAL GOVERNMENT

The local government system comprises five county borough corporations, five borough corporations in the major cities, and 29 county councils, as well as numerous urban district councils and boards of town commissioners. Each of these is elected at regular intervals by universal adult suffrage. Of the 29 county councils, only 24 represent whole counties. For administrative purposes, the traditional County Tipperary is divided into a North Riding and a South Riding, each having a county council, and Dublin also is divided, among three county councils (Dún Laoghaire-Rathdown, Fingal, and South Dublin). County councils and county borough corporations are responsible for physical planning, roads, sewerage and water supplies, housing, public libraries, fire services, and courthouses. Local government authorities in the republic have no functions in relation to police or education

Important policy decisions (e.g., on local taxes, borrowing, and the making of bylaws) are made by the elected councils. Administration, on the other hand, is the responsibility of the county (or city) manager, who usually consults with members of the council before discharging important executive functions. There is a city manager for each county borough council, and for each county council there is a county manager, who also acts as manager for the lesser local authorities within the county. Noncounty boroughs, urban districts, and towns have more limited duties, and, in regard to functions outside their scope, they form part of the administrative counties in which they are situated. The local government system is supervised by the national Department of the Environment.

JUSTICE

Irish law is based on common law as modified by subsequent legislation and by the constitution. Judges are appointed by the president and normally serve for life or until retirement. They may be removed from office only in the case of incapacity or "stated misbehaviour" and then only by resolution of both houses of the Oireachtas.

COMMON LAW

Common law is a body of law that is based on custom and general principles and that, embodied in case law, serves as precedent or is applied to situations not covered by statute. Under the common-law system, when a court decides and reports its decision concerning a particular case, the case becomes part of the body of law and can be used in later cases involving similar matters. This use of precedents is known as stare decisis. Common law has been administered in the courts of England since the Middle Ages; it is also found in the U.S. and in most of the British Commonwealth. It is distinguished from civil law.

There are district courts and circuit courts, as well as a High Court and a Supreme Court that acts as the court of final appeal. The Supreme Court consists of the chief justice and seven other judges. The circuit courts have jurisdiction to try all serious offenses except murder, treason, and piracy. Criminal trials, which take place before a jury, can be held in a circuit court or in the central criminal court (a division of the High Court). A special criminal court was established in 1972 with jurisdiction over cases of terrorism.

POLITICAL PROCESS

All citizens 18 years of age or older are eligible to vote. Members of both the Seanad and Dáil are chosen at least once every five years. The members of the Dáil are elected in three- to five-member constituencies by single transferable vote, a form of proportional representation. Of the 60 members of the Seanad, 11 are appointed by the prime minister, 6 are elected by the Irish universities, and 43 are elected to represent various economic, vocational, and cultural interests. Women have made significant political gains. Although during the 1990s women won only about one-eighth of the seats in the Dáil and comprised about one-fifth of the Seanad, the country twice elected female presidents, Mary Robinson in 1990 and Mary McAleese in 1997. However, with the proportion of women in the Oireachtas remaining at roughly the same levels in the early 21st century, there were some calls for the introduction of quotas for female representation.

The major political parties are Fianna Fáil, Fine Gael, the Labour Party, and Sinn Fein (the last of which is mostly associated with Northern Ireland politics but has made entrees into Irish electoral politics, including seeing its leader, Gerry Adams, elected to the Dáil in 2011). Independents also have a significant presence in the Dáil. Fianna Fáil, a republican party, was founded by Eamon de Valera, who opposed the Anglo-Irish Treaty of 1921. The party boycotted the Dáil until 1927 but won the general election of 1932, when de Valera became prime minister, a position he held, with two intermissions, until 1959, when he was elected president. Fine Gael is the party of the Irish nationalists Arthur Griffith, Michael Collins, and William Thomas Cosgrave, who supported the treaty of 1921 and founded the Irish Free State. Cumann na nGaedheal, forerunner of Fine Gael, held power from 1922 to 1932. After World War II, government leadership tended to shift between Fine Gael–Labour Party coalitions and Fianna Fáil. Fianna Fáil formed several independent (i.e., noncoalition) governments until the late 1980s, when it entered into an alliance with the Progressive Democrats. Later governing coalitions were led by both parties. During the 1990s all major parties accepted the position within the United Kingdom of Northern Ireland. The Irish constitution was altered to acknowledge this fact in 1999, when voters overwhelmingly endorsed the Good Friday Agreement

MICHAEL COLLINS

A hero of the Irish struggle for independence, Michael Collins (born October 16, 1890, Woodfield, Sam's Cross, County Cork, Ireland—died August 22, 1922, Béal-na-mBlath, Cork) is best remembered for his daring strategy in directing the campaign of guerrilla warfare during the intensification of the Anglo-Irish War (1919–21).

Collins worked as a clerk in London from 1906 until he returned to Ireland in 1916. He fought in the Easter Rising, was arrested and held in detention at Frongoch, Merioneth, but was released in December 1916. In December 1918 he was one of 27 out of 73 elected Sinn Féin members (most of whom were in jail) present when Dáil Éireann (Irish Assembly) convened in Dublin and declared for the republic. Their elected president, Eamon de Valera, and vice president, Arthur Griffith, were both in prison. Hence, much responsibility fell on Collins, who became first the Dáil's minister of home affairs and, after arranging for de Valera's escape from Lincoln jail (February 1919), minister of finance. It was as director of intelligence of the Irish Republican Army (IRA), how-

Michael Collins, 1919. Encyclopædia Britannica, Inc.

ever, that he became famous. As chief planner and coordinator of the revolutionary movement, Collins organized numerous attacks on police and the assassination in November 1920 of many of Britain's leading intelligence agents in Ireland. He headed the list of men wanted by the British, who placed a price of £10,000 on his head.

After the truce of July 1921, Griffith and Collins were sent to London by de Valera as the principal negotiators for peace (October–December 1921). The treaty of December 6, 1921, was signed by Collins in the belief that it was the best that could be obtained for Ireland at the time and in the full awareness that he might be signing his own death warrant. It gave Ireland dominion status, but its provision for an oath of allegiance to the British crown was unacceptable to de Valera and other republican leaders. Collins's persuasiveness helped win acceptance for the treaty by a small majority in the Dáil, and a provisional government was formed under his chairmanship, but effective administration was obstructed by the mutinous activities of the anti-treaty republicans. Collins refrained from taking action against his former comrades until IRA insurgents seized the Four Courts in Dublin and civil war became inevitable. William Thomas Cosgrave replaced Collins as chairman when the latter assumed command of the army in mid-July 1922 in order to crush the insurgency. About five weeks later, while on a tour of military inspection, Collins was shot to death by anti-treaty insurgents in an ambush in west Cork.

(Belfast Agreement) of 1998, a peace plan signed by the Irish and British governments and nationalist (Roman Catholic) and unionist (Protestant) political parties in Northern Ireland.

SECURITY

Ireland has no local police forces. The Guardians of the Peace (An Garda Síochána), established in 1922, is a nationwide force headed by a commissioner who is responsible to the minister for justice. A few hundred members of the force are assigned to detective duties; they are usually plainclothes officers and, when necessary, are armed. The rest of the force is uniformed and does not carry firearms.

Ireland's defense forces, which include both active-duty and reserve components, are made up largely of army personnel, although the country also maintains small naval and air forces. Under the constitution, the president is the supreme commander of the armed forces; however, the prime minister effectively oversees the military through the minister for defense and a defense council. Irish forces, including the air corps and the naval service, have played an active part in United Nations (UN) peacekeeping operations. In the late 20th century Irish officers or forces served in UN missions to such places as Lebanon and other areas of the Middle East, Afghanistan, Congo (Kinshasa), Cyprus, and the Balkans. There is no conscription; enlistment in the defense forces and the reserve force is voluntary. Ireland has struggled with its dual commitments to its historical tradition of neutrality and to its obligations to the European Union, which include defense elements.

HEALTH AND WELFARE

Health services are administered by eight regional health boards under the general supervision of the Department of Health and Children. Health examinations, child welfare clinics, and the treatment of tuberculosis and other infectious diseases are available to all without charge. Otherwise, the cost of public health services depends on the patient's means. Persons who cannot afford to pay are entitled to a comprehensive health service free of charge. A middle-income group—insured workers, smaller farmers, and others of restricted means—is entitled to a free maternity and child welfare service and to free hospital and specialist services. Those who are more affluent normally arrange and pay for their own

IRISH SWEEPSTAKES

One of the world's largest lotteries, the Irish Sweepstakes (formally known as the Irish Hospitals' Sweepstakes) was authorized by the Irish government in 1930 to benefit Irish hospitals. A private trust was formed to run the lottery and market tickets throughout the world. During the 57 years of its existence, the contest derived more revenue from the United States than from any other country, although all the tickets sold there were smuggled in and sold illegally. There was much counterfeiting of tickets, seldom detectable because the purchaser had no further interest in the ticket if it was not a winning ticket.

Ticket stubs were returned to Ireland to be drawn from a barrel and matched with the name of a horse running in a major Irish or British race. The largest prizes went to ticket holders whose horses won, placed, or showed. A state lottery replaced the Irish Sweepstakes in 1987.

medical advice and hospital services, but a voluntary health insurance program was established by law in 1957. Owing in large measure to the world-famous Irish Hospitals' Sweepstakes (1930–87), a large lottery that was promoted internationally, the republic developed an excellent system of hospitals.

Pay-related social insurance is paid by most employees age 16 and over. Benefits include widows' and orphans' pensions, unemployment and disability benefits, deserted wives' allowances, and old-age pensions. The indigent receive certain benefits on a noncontributory basis. These include widows' and orphans' pensions, old-age pensions, home assistance, unemployment assistance, and pensions for those disabled or blind. Children's allowances are paid to all households for each child under age 16, irrespective of means.

Ireland is a signatory to international agreements on human rights, and capital punishment has been outlawed. Because of the influence of the Roman Catholic church, Ireland historically has had strict social laws (e.g., abortion is illegal). However, referenda in the 1980s and '90s resulted in some reforms, including the legalization of divorce and contraception. In 2010 the European Court on Human Rights found Ireland's abortion policies to be in violation of European standards of human rights.

HOUSING

Compared with much of western Europe, Ireland has very high rates of home ownership. Whereas less than one-tenth of units were owned by their occupants when the country became independent in 1922, by the beginning of the 21st century roughly four-fifths of units were owner-occupied. The housing stock in the country is relatively modern, with many units built

Houses in Eyeries, County Cork. © Glen Allison/Getty Images

since the 1970s. However, there have been housing shortages, and the waiting list for public housing units nearly doubled during the 1990s. Meanwhile, prices for homes rose dramatically as home ownership became a largely unfunded property bubble that played an important role in the Irish financial crisis of 2008. In the wake of that crisis, housing prices fell precipitously.

EDUCATION

Primary education is free, compulsory, and almost entirely religious denominational. There are several state-aided teachers' training colleges. The secondary school system comprises private schools that are predominantly owned by religious communities but that receive most of their funding from the state; comprehensive

UNIVERSITY OF DUBLIN

The oldest institution of higher education in Ireland, the University of Dublin (also called Trinity College), was founded in 1592 by Queen Elizabeth I of England and Ireland and endowed by the city of Dublin. When founded, it was intended that Trinity College would be the first of many constituent colleges of the University of Dublin. No other colleges were established, however, and the two names became interchangeable. The full benefits of the university—degrees, fellowships, scholarships, and emoluments—were limited to Anglicans for many years, but in 1873 all religious requirements were eliminated. The university library contains many illuminated manuscripts, including the famous Book of Kells.

The University of Dublin (Trinity College), Dublin. Holger Leue/Tourism Ireland

and community schools, which are completely state-owned; and vocational schools, which provide academic as well as vocational courses leading to qualifications in architecture, accountancy, engineering, computing, electronics, and similar professions. There is also a growing number of multi-denominational private schools in Ireland operated by the Educate Together organization. The vocational education system includes schools of art, music, domestic science, and hotel training. A number of regional technical colleges provide advanced vocational courses. Students graduating from the state-aided teachers' training colleges often receive university degrees. University education is provided at the University of Dublin (Trinity College), founded in 1592, and at the National University of Ireland, founded in 1908. The latter has constituent universities at Dublin, Cork, Galway, and Maynooth, as well as several associated colleges. In 1989 the national institutes for higher education in Limerick and Dublin, which emphasized applied studies in varied, flexible course structures, were given university status and renamed the University of Limerick and the Dublin City University. The Higher Education Authority was established in 1972 to deal with the financial and organizational problems of higher education.

Education is highly valued in Ireland, which is sometimes called the "Land of Saints and Scholars," and the strength of Irish education was often cited as a major contributor to the takeoff of the Celtic Tiger economy in the late 1980s and 1990s. However, concerns about the Irish education system were raised when Ireland's national literacy ranking fell from 5th in the world in 2000 to 17th in 2010. At the same time, Ireland continues to see its higher education as a major asset, and the government has emphasized research and development as part of its attempt to create a sustainable economy.

CHAPTER 5

CULTURAL LIFE

The cultural milieu of Ireland has been shaped by the dynamic interplay between the ancient Celtic traditions of the people and those imposed on them from outside, notably from Britain. This has produced a culture of rich, distinctive character in which the use of language—be it Irish or English—has always been the central element. Not surprisingly, Irish culture is best known through its literature, drama, and songs; above all, the Irish are renowned as masters of the art of conversation.

Use of the Irish language declined steadily during the 19th century and was nearly wiped out by the Irish Potato Famine of the 1840s and subsequent emigration, which particularly affected the Irish-speaking population in the western portion of the country—the area "beyond the pale" (i.e., beyond the English-speaking and English-controlled area around Dublin). From the mid-19th century, in the years following the famine, there was a resurgence in Irish language and traditional culture. This Gaelic revival led, in turn, to the Irish literary renaissance of the late 19th and early 20th centuries, in which native expression was explored and renewed by a generation of writers and academics. It also produced a resurgence in traditional musical and dance forms. The cultural revivalism became an inspiration to the Irish nationalist struggle of the early decades of the 20th century. Partly because of government subsidies and programs, traditional cultural activities, especially the use of the Irish language and the revival of arts and crafts, have increased.

DAILY LIFE AND SOCIAL CUSTOMS

Ireland has several distinct regional cultures, rather than a single national one; moreover, the daily lives of city dwellers are in some ways much different from those living in the countryside. For example, whereas Dublin is one of Europe's most cosmopolitan cities, the Blasket Islands of Dingle Bay, off Ireland's southwestern coast, seem almost a throwback to earlier centuries. Wherever they live, the Irish maintain a vibrant and lively folk culture. Thousands participate in the country's numerous amateur musical, dance, and storytelling events. A great many also engage in a variety of craft-based industries, producing items such as glass, ceramics, ironwork, woodturning, linens, embroidery, and knitwear, served by the Crafts Council of Ireland (based in Kilkenny) and an annual trade fair in Dublin. Irish fashion has advanced beyond the still-popular Aran sweater, with various designers establishing fashion trends that have broad appeal both nationally and internationally.

The Irish pub serves as a focal point for many small villages and urban neighbourhoods, a place where the great Irish passion for conversation, stories, and jokes can be indulged. Pub attendance declined somewhat in the early 21st century after the imposition of a smoking ban, the restriction of hours when families could bring children to eat at pubs, and the enactment of more-stringent drunk- driving laws. Still, Ireland remains home to some of the world's finest beers, whiskeys, and other spirits, which accompany the lively music and socializing that seem to come naturally to the Irish and those who visit. Traditional Irish music—using locally made instruments such as the fiddle, the tin whistle, and the uilleann pipes (Irish bagpipes)—is performed at many pubs, and traditional songs are often sung there in the Gaelic language, at times accompanied by the Celtic harp (an emblem of Ireland). The *céilí*, a traditional musical gathering, is an enduring expression of Irish social life that has counterparts in other Celtic cultures. Such gatherings, as well as hiring fairs, cattle shows, and other festivals, usually feature locally produced ales and whiskeys and traditional foods such as soda bread, corned beef, and colcannon (a stew of potatoes and cabbage).

The Wexford Opera Festival, held annually in the fall, draws a large international audience. Of particular importance is St. Patrick's Day (March 17), honouring the country's patron saint. Whereas overseas the holiday has become a boisterous, largely secular celebration of all things Irish, in Ireland it is a religious occasion often observed by saying prayers for peace, especially in neighbouring Northern Ireland. Nevertheless, some of the practices celebrated abroad have been adopted locally in the interest of tourism.

THE ARTS

If Ireland's contribution to the arts were limited to the works of satirist Jonathan Swift, novelist James Joyce, playwrights George Bernard Shaw and Samuel Beckett, and poets William Butler Yeats and Seamus Heaney, it would already be of inestimable value, but these are only the

SAINT PATRICK'S DAY

Celebrated on March 17, Saint Patrick's Day is the feast day of St. Patrick, patron saint of Ireland. Born in Roman Britain in the late 4th century, he was kidnapped at the age of 16 and taken to Ireland as a slave. He escaped but returned about 432 to convert the Irish to Christianity. By the time of his death on March 17, 461, he had established monasteries, churches, and schools. Many legends grew up around him—for example, that he drove the snakes out of Ireland and used the shamrock to explain the Trinity. Ireland came to celebrate his day with religious services and feasts.

It was emigrants, particularly to the United States, who transformed St. Patrick's Day into a largely secular holiday of revelry and celebration of things Irish. Cities with large numbers

Children at the Saint Patrick's Day parade in Dublin. Tourism Ireland

of Irish immigrants, who often wielded political power, staged the most extensive celebrations, which included elaborate parades. Boston held its first St. Patrick's Day parade in 1737, followed by New York City in 1762. Since 1962 Chicago has coloured its river green to mark the holiday. (Although blue was the colour traditionally associated with St. Patrick, green is now commonly connected with the day.) Irish and non-Irish alike commonly participate in the "wearing of the green"—sporting an item of green clothing or a shamrock, the Irish national plant, in the lapel. Corned beef and cabbage are associated with the holiday, and even beer is sometimes dyed green to celebrate the day. Although some of these practices eventually were adopted by the Irish themselves, they did so largely for the benefit of tourists.

most famous of the many Irish artists who have made their mark on world culture. Moreover, this short list includes neither musicians nor visual artists, such as the Clancy Brothers and U2, painter Francis Bacon, and filmmaker Neil Jordan.

LITERATURE: PROSE AND POETRY

The earliest known literature in the Old Irish language takes several forms. Many manuscripts, such as the Milan and Turin glosses on the Bible (so named for the libraries where they are housed), are religious in nature; others are secular and include lyric poems, fragments of epic verse, and riddles. Little of this literature is read today except by scholars of the Irish language and of comparative historical linguistics. Instead, the stream of Irish literature that has enriched world culture has been almost entirely written in English. The sheer volume of work attributed to Irish writers is remarkable considering the country's small size and, until relatively recently, its only partially literate populace.

A flowering of Irish literary works especially occurred with the standardization of Irish in the mid-20th century. After World War II a new wave of poets, novelists, and dramatists produced a significant literature in modern Irish, among them Máirtín Ó Cadhain, Máirtín Ó Direáin, and Máire Mhac an tSaoi. Beginning in the 1970s, another generation of writers made important contributions in Irish, notably Mícheál Ó Siadhail, Gabriel Rosenstock, Michael Hartnett, Nuala Ní Dhomhnaill, Áine Ní Ghlinn, and Cathal Ó Searcaigh.

Many modes of thought and expression characteristic of Irish-language formulations were gradually absorbed into the English spoken in Ireland. The remarkable contribution that Anglo-Irish literature and drama have made to the Western world may in part be ascribed to this linguistic cross-fertilization. It is also noteworthy that so small a country should produce so much creative literary genius. The great Anglo-Irish satirist Jonathan Swift, dean of St. Patrick's Cathedral, Dublin, drew upon his experience of

JAMES JOYCE

Irish novelist James Joyce (born February 2, 1882, Dublin—died January 13, 1941, Zürich, Switzerland) decided early in his life to become a writer. He was educated at a Jesuit school (though he soon rejected Roman Catholicism) and at University College, Dublin, and in 1902 he moved to Paris, which would become his principal home after years spent in Trieste and Zürich. His life was difficult, marked by financial troubles, chronic eye diseases that occasionally left him totally blind, censorship problems, and his daughter Lucia's mental illness. The remarkable story collection *The Dubliners* (1914) and the autobiographical novel *Portrait of the Artist as a Young Man* (1916), his early prose volumes, were powerful examples of his gift for storytelling and his great intelligence. With financial help from friends and supporters, including Ezra Pound (1885–1972), Sylvia Beach (1887–1962), and Harriet Shaw Weaver (1876–1961), he spent seven years writing *Ulysses* (1922), the controversial masterpiece (initially banned in the U.S. and Britain) now widely regarded by many as the greatest English-language novel of the 20th century. It embodies a highly experimental use of language and exploration of such new literary methods as interior monologue and stream-of-consciousness narrative. He spent 17 years on his final work, the extraordinary *Finnegans Wake* (1939), famous for its complex and demanding linguistic virtuosity.

James Joyce, oil on canvas by Jacques-Émile Blanche, 1935. DEA Picture Library/De Agostini/Getty Images

life in Ireland for his writing. The list of influential Irish prose writers and poets who both benefited from and contributed to the interplay between the different strands of the Anglo-Irish tradition is long. Among them are two of Ireland's four winners of the Nobel Prize for Literature, the poets William Butler Yeats (1923) and Seamus Heaney (1995). Others with an international reputation include prose writers George Moore, Elizabeth Bowen, Flann O'Brien, Edna O'Brien, William Trevor, John McGahern, Roddy Doyle, John Banville, Jennifer Johnston, and especially James Joyce; and poets John Montague (American-born), Eavan Boland, Brendan Kennelly, Paul Durcan, and Paula Meehan. The Irish Writers' Centre and Poetry Ireland actively promote contemporary literature in prose and verse.

THEATRE

Irish achievements in the theatre rival those in literature. Two Irish dramatists won Nobel Prizes for Literature, George Bernard Shaw (1925) and Samuel Beckett (1969), and several others, including Oliver Goldsmith, Richard Brinsley Sheridan, Oscar Wilde, John Millington Synge, and Sean O'Casey, are also known throughout the English-speaking world.

Dublin is the centre of Ireland's theatrical life. Its Abbey Theatre, founded in 1904 and rebuilt in the mid-1960s, stages classic Irish plays, as well as new works in both Irish and English. The Gate Theatre produces Irish and international drama, while the Peacock Theatre, located under the foyer of the Abbey Theatre, concentrates on experimental plays and on works in Irish. Theatres and theatre companies

ABBEY THEATRE

Dublin's Abbey Theatre is one of the most renowned theatrical establishments in the world. It grew out of the Irish Literary Theatre (founded in 1899 by William Butler Yeats and Isabella Augusta, Lady Gregory, and devoted to fostering Irish poetic drama), which in 1902 was taken over by the Irish National Dramatic Society, led by W.G. and Frank J. Fay and formed to present Irish actors in Irish plays. In 1903 this became the Irish National Theatre Society, with which many leading figures of the Irish literary renaissance were closely associated. The quality of its productions was quickly recognized, and in 1904 an Englishwoman, Annie Horniman, a friend of Yeats, paid for the conversion of an old theatre in Abbey Street, Dublin, into the Abbey Theatre. The Abbey opened in December of that year with a bill of plays by Yeats, Lady Gregory, and John Millington Synge (who joined the other two as codirector). Founder members included the Fays, Arthur Sinclair, and Sara Allgood.

The Abbey's staging of Synge's satire *The Playboy of the Western World*, on January 26, 1907, stirred up so much resentment in the audience over its portrayal of the Irish peasantry that there was a riot. When the Abbey players toured the United States for the first time in 1911, similar protests and disorders were provoked when the play opened in New York City and Philadelphia.

The years 1907–09 were difficult times for the Abbey. Changes in personnel affected the management of the theatre, and the Fay brothers, whose commitment to nationalistic and folk drama conflicted with Yeats's art-theatre outlook, departed for the United States. Horniman withdrew her financial support, and the management of the theatre changed hands several times with little success until the post was filled by the playwright-director Lennox Robinson in 1910. The onset of World War I and the Irish Rebellion of 1916 almost caused the closing of the theatre. Its luck changed, however, in 1924, when it became the first state-subsidized theatre in the English-speaking world. The emergence of the playwright Sean O'Casey also stimulated new life in the theatre, and from 1923 to 1926 the Abbey staged three of his plays: *The Shadow of a Gunman*, *Juno and the Paycock*, and *The Plough and the Stars*, the last a provocative dramatization of the Easter Rising of 1916. In the early 1950s the Abbey company moved to the nearby Queen's Theatre after a fire had destroyed its playhouse. A new Abbey Theatre, housing a smaller, experimental theatre, was completed in 1966 on the original site. While the Abbey today retains its traditional focus on Irish plays, it also stages a wide range of classic and new works from around the world.

such as Galway's Druid Theatre are found throughout the country, however, promoting a wide range of national and international drama. In addition, there is a vigorous amateur dramatic movement active throughout the country.

MUSIC AND DANCE

Irish traditional musical forms date from preliterate times. The Irish harp long had been the only instrument played, but many other instruments—such as the uilleann pipes, fiddle, and accordion—were added later. The Royal Irish Academy of Music is a major institution for music training, and folkloric and musical conservation groups such as Comhaltas Ceoltóirí Éireann (Fellowship of Irish Musicians) have established workshops and libraries throughout the country and around the world. The revival of traditional music in the late 19th and early 20th centuries was followed by an even more energetic resurgence beginning in the 1960s. Irish songs gained wide appeal in Europe in the 19th century, and the music brought to the United States by Irish immigrants became one of the principal sources of traditional American music. Irish traditional musicians such as the Clancy Brothers, Planxty, the Boys of the Lough, Clannad, and the Chieftains have toured much of the world. More urban and working-class-based music and song have been represented by groups such as the Dubliners and the Wolfe Tones. Interest in Irish traditional music was greatly boosted by a vogue for Irish pubs that spread across the world. Elements of traditional Irish music have also been appropriated by rock musicians to create a distinctive Irish popular music form with great international appeal. For example, beginning in the 1980s, the postpunk group U2 received international acclaim, and its lead singer, Bono, gained fame for his outspokenness on domestic and global political issues. Other popular music groups and artists have included Thin Lizzy, Rory Gallagher, the Corrs, the Cranberries, Bob Geldof, Sinéad O'Connor, Mary and Frances Black, and Hothouse Flowers. Similarly influenced by traditional Irish music, the ethereal-voiced New Age singer Enya (Eithne Ní Bhraonáin) gained a huge international following beginning in the late 1980s. Opera is less popular in Ireland, although singers such as Bernadette Greevy and Suzanne Murphy have gained widespread recognition. Among the newer Irish artists who have come to the forefront in the 21st century are vocalist Sharon Shannon, the traditional group Danú, and the pop duo Jedward.

Ireland is famous for its tenor singers of Irish traditional tunes. The prototypical Irish tenor was John McCormack, noted for his brilliant tone and resonant timbre. Although the fashion faded from roughly the 1930s to the 1960s, it

U2

By the end of the 1980s the Irish rock group U2 had established itself as one of the world's most popular and innovative bands. The four young men who would become U2 —Bono (born Paul Hewson; May 10, 1960, Dublin), the Edge (born David Evans; August 8, 1961, Barking, England), Adam Clayton (born March 13, 1960, Oxford, Oxfordshire, England), and Larry Mullen, Jr. (born October 31, 1961, Dublin)—were classmates at a Dublin secondary school when they began playing together, undeterred by their initial lack of musicianship. The band's first recordings brought compassion, tenderness, and spirituality to their consideration of social and political issues such as the civil strife in Northern Ireland. The group's inspirational live performances made it a word-of-mouth sensation long before it began its regular assault on the top of pop charts. But, with the multimillion-selling success of *The Joshua Tree* album (1987) and the number-one hits "With or Without You" and "I Still Haven't Found What I'm Looking For," the members of U2 became huge pop stars.

With *Achtung Baby* (1991) U2 reinvented itself for a new decade. The album, which offered a sound heavily influenced by European experimental, electronic, and disco music, was accompanied by a stage show suffused with uncharacteristic irony and self-deprecating humour. The 1992 Zoo TV tour was even more extraordinary, presenting nothing less than one of the most technically ambitious and artistically accomplished large-scale rock shows ever mounted. Yet the flashy presentation belied the band's ongoing interest with matters of the soul. Even as U2 immersed itself in techno textures, it explored the dehumanizing aspects of media and technology.

U2 performing on Saturday Night Live, 2009. PRNewsFoto/Live Nation/AP Images

With the dawn of the new millennium, the band underwent another reinvention, but this time it was a return to its roots on the appropriately titled *All That You Can't Leave Behind* (2000) and on *How to Dismantle an Atomic Bomb* (2004). Atmosphere and mystery took a backseat to riffs and songcraft as U2 once more became a huge commercial force. In 2009 the band released its 12th studio album, *No Line on the Horizon*, which featured enhanced roles for longtime collaborators Brian Eno and Daniel Lanois; the layered textures of the group's most experimental work recurred across the album. Bono and the Edge also contributed the music and lyrics to the musical *Spider-Man: Turn Off the Dark*, one of the most expensive in Broadway history, which opened in 2011.

regained its vitality and popularity in the work of Frank Patterson and American-born Robert White.

Best-known of the Irish classical composers are John Field, whose work influenced that of Frédéric Chopin, and Michael Balfe. Based in Dublin and maintained by Radio Telefís Éireann (RTÉ; the state-owned broadcasting company), the RTÉ National Symphony Orchestra and the RTÉ Concert Orchestra are the country's principal orchestral groups. Ireland's leading contemporary music ensemble, Concorde, commissions and performs the work of contemporary composers. New music is supported by the Contemporary Music Centre in Dublin, a national archive and resource centre. Many arts organizations and individual artists are supported in part by the Arts Council of Ireland, a developmental government agency.

Ireland has a long tradition of folk dancing. Solo dancing is characterized by its lightning footwork and high kicks, all executed while the upper body is kept rigidly straight; jigs and reels have always been popular. The interest in Irish dancing, which grew apace with the revival of traditional music, led in the 1990s to the creation of the performance work *Riverdance*, which achieved international acclaim and sparked the founding of dance companies around the world that explored this style.

VISUAL ARTS

At the turn of the 20th century, Irish art remained relatively isolated from the contemporary trends that spread throughout Europe. Painter John Butler Yeats (father of poet William Butler Yeats) received widespread praise for his portraiture, as did Sir William Orpen, who influenced a generation of Irish artists as a teacher. Paul Henry's depictions of the Irish countryside were also popular. Jack Butler Yeats, the poet's brother, using traditional Irish subjects and elements of Celtic mythology, became recognized as the major Irish artist of the mid-20th century.

It was only after World War II that avant-garde developments, popular in the rest of Europe for decades, fully touched Irish art. In this climate, Louis Le Brocquy gained fame for his abstract portraits. Perhaps the most prominent Irish-born artist of the postwar period was Francis Bacon, who became known for his brutal figurative paintings. Although he spent most of his life in Britain, his studio has been reconstructed in the Hugh Lane Gallery (formally Dublin City Gallery The Hugh Lane) in Dublin. Throughout the postwar period, alternative exhibiting spaces and organizations increasingly made it possible for more experimental styles and artists to be noticed in Ireland.

By the late 20th century, Irish art reflected a wide range of styles and media. As in literature, many contemporary visual artists (e.g., Brian Maguire, Dorothy Cross, Kathy Pendergast, and Brian Bourke) gained international reputations, with their work included in major international shows such as the Venice Biennale. Many late-century Irish artists settled in the thriving art scene in London, yet their work often remained infused with the social and political issues of their homeland.

Annual art exhibitions, the most important of which is the Royal Hibernian Academy, are a regular feature of modern Irish cultural life, and many corporate collections of contemporary Irish art are of the highest calibre. Printmaking has

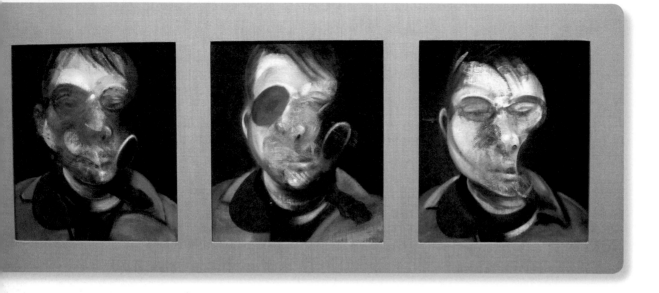

A Francis Bacon triptych showing three studies for a self-portrait. Bacon's largely figural works are known for their distorted, isolated, and even brutal feel. Mario Tama/Getty Images

flourished since the establishment of the Graphic Studio and Graphic Studio Gallery by Mary Farl Powers, followed by the Black Church Print Studio (both now located in Dublin) and other studios in urban areas.

Film is also an important medium for Irish visual artists and writers. During the late 20th century, several Irish films received international acclaim, including *The Crying Game* (1992), which won an Academy Award for best screenplay, *My Left Foot* (1989), and *In the Name of the Father* (1993). *The Magdalene Sisters* (2002) considered the abuses of young women in the Roman Catholic Church in Ireland's not-too-distant past. *Once* (2006) brought a lighter mood with its focus on the musical life of Dublin but also on the new multiculturalism of the city. Meanwhile, a stream of Irish actors and directors have made an imprint on the global film industry, including directors Jim Sheridan and Neil Jordan, and actors Gabriel Byrne, Colin Farrell, Brenda Fricker, Brendan Gleeson, Richard Harris, Colm Meany, Maureen O'Hara, and Saoirse Ronan. International films such as *The Quiet Man* (1952), *Ryan's Daughter* (1970), *The Dead* (1987), *The Secret of Roan Inish* (1994), *Michael Collins* (1996), *Angela's Ashes* (1999), and *The Wind That Shakes the Barley* (2006) have also focused on Irish themes and history.

The endeavours of the Irish Georgian Society and of An Taisce (the National

Trust) have helped to protect the architectural heritage of the country. Dublin's many 18th-century buildings are among the finest-preserved in all of Europe.

CULTURAL INSTITUTIONS

Most of the country's major museums, libraries, and learned societies are located in Dublin, including the National Museum of Ireland, the National Gallery of Ireland, the Irish Museum of Modern Art (IMMA), and the National Library of Ireland. Under British rule a number of Anglo-Irish cultural institutions were established there and successfully adapted to accommodate stronger nationalist sentiment during the 20th century. These include the Royal Irish Academy (1785) and the Royal Dublin Society (1731). Also important are the Royal Hibernian Academy (1823) and the Royal Irish Academy of Music (1856). The quasi-governmental Arts Council (An Chomhairle Ealaíon; 1951) distributes annual state grants to assist the arts and artists. Individual writers, artists, and composers also are aided by tax concessions and by additional financial support from the Aosdána organization. The establishment of a national lottery in 1986 substantially increased funding for the arts and for sports.

Many institutions are specifically concerned with the popularization and preservation of aspects of traditional national culture. Notably, the Gaelic League (Conradh na Gaeilge; 1893)

This sand sculpture titled The Elements: Air, on display at Dublin Castle in 2009, was created by Duthain Dealbh (Gaelic: Fleeting Sculpture), a group that also works in snow, ice, and fire. Hope Lourie Killcoyne

promotes the use of the Irish language. Other bodies concentrate on the organization of folk music festivals (*feiseanna*), at which there are competitions in traditional storytelling and dancing as well as in instrumental music and singing.

SPORTS AND RECREATION

The Irish are avid sports fans, especially of their native games of Gaelic football—a cross between football (soccer) and rugby—and hurling, which resembles a rough-and-tumble version of field hockey. Both are promoted by the Gaelic Athletic Association (GAA; Cumann Lúthchleas), founded in 1884 to revive native Irish sports. Today there are several hundred thousand members of the GAA who play these games as amateurs, and the professional teams compete in the All-Ireland matches that draw huge crowds to Dublin's Croke Park. Handball is also a traditional Irish sport.

Football and rugby are widely popular, often played in sold-out stadiums in Dublin. In 1990 the national football team reached the quarterfinals in the World Cup, and Irish players are prominent on the rosters of professional teams throughout the world. The Irish are extremely

HURLING

There is considerable reference to hurling (*iomáin* in Gaelic), the national pastime, in the oldest Irish manuscripts, describing the game as far back as the 13th century BCE; many heroes of ancient tales were expert hurlers. The stick used is called a hurley, *camán* in Gaelic, and *camáns* in relief decorate some monuments to 15th-century chieftains. Hurling was for long a game played between neighbouring clans or rival parishes with unlimited numbers of players on either side.

In 1884 the Gaelic Athletic Association was founded in Thurles, County Tipperary, to revive and standardize hurling and other traditional Irish pastimes.

The hurley, or *camán*, resembling a hockey stick except that the head is shorter and wider, is made of young pliable ash, 3.5 feet (1.07 m) long and 3 inches (7.6 centimetres) wide in the oval-shaped

Hurling has been played in Ireland for a good thousand years. Here, three players keep up the tradition at a hurling match in Kilkenny, County Kilkenny, in southeast Ireland. Ingolf Pompe/LOOK/Getty Images

striking blade. The width of the blade enables the ball to be hit overhead from man to man as well as along the ground. Each team consists of 15 players. The average pitch, or field, is 150 yards (137 m) long and 90 yards (82 m) wide. Goalposts at each end are 21 feet (6.4 metres) high and 21 feet apart with a crossbar 8 feet (2.4 m) above the ground. A point is scored by hitting the ball over the opposing crossbar. A goal, scored by driving the ball under the crossbar, is three points. The ball, or *sliothar,* has a cork centre, wound with wool and covered with leather, and is 9–10 inches (22.9–25.4 cm) in circumference. It may be caught in the hand before hitting but not thrown or lifted; it may also be juggled or carried on the blade of the stick or may be hit from left or right. There is a women's version of the game, called camogie.

passionate about horse racing, and the Irish Derby draws Europe's best competitors to The Curragh, the flat racetrack in County Kildare. Greyhound racing at Shelbourne Park in Dublin is also well attended. In bicycling, Dubliner Steven Roche won the Tour de France and the World Championship in 1987.

The Olympic Council of Ireland was formed in 1922, and Ireland's official participation in the Olympic Games began in Paris in 1924. (Irish athletes had competed for Great Britain in previous games, since 1896.) Since then Ireland has missed only the 1936 games. The first medal by an Irishman came in 1896, when John Boland won a gold medal in tennis for Great Britain. The first medal for the Irish team came in 1928 in Amsterdam, where Patrick O'Callaghan won a gold in the hammer throw. In 1996 Michelle Smith became the first Irish female athlete to win a gold medal, capturing three gold medals in swimming, though she was later banned for four years from competition after being found guilty of manipulating a drug-test sample. Four years later distance runner Sonia O'Sullivan won a silver medal in the 5,000-metre event at the 2000 Olympic Games. Irish competitors won five medals in the 2012 London Olympics, including Katie Taylor, who won a gold medal in women's boxing.

MEDIA AND PUBLISHING

Several daily newspapers are published in Ireland, including some that have a national circulation. Leading dailies include the *Irish Independent* and *The Irish Times* of Dublin and the *Irish Examiner* of Cork. There also are a large number of regional weekly papers. Dublin is the centre of the publishing industry, and nearly all of the republic's periodicals are based there.

RTÉ, the national state-owned radio and television broadcaster, began radio service in 1926 and television service in 1961. A second RTÉ national television channel, Network 2, was launched in 1978. RTÉ is financed by revenue from license fees and advertising and is governed by the government-appointed RTÉ Authority. There is an extensive independent radio network with many privately owned stations; an independent Irish-language television station, TG4 (Teilifís na Gaeilge), was established in 1996. The population also receives broadcasts from the United Kingdom and other European countries and can subscribe to cable and satellite services. In 1998 a privately owned commercial television channel, TV3, commenced operations; in 2008, it acquired Channel 6, another privately owned channel that had begun broadcasting in 2006, and subsequently rebranded it as 3e. The regulation of television broadcasting is one of the responsibilities of the Broadcasting Authority of Ireland.

CHAPTER 6

EARLY IRELAND

The human occupation of Ireland did not begin until a late stage in the prehistory of Europe. It generally was held that the first arrivals to Ireland were Mesolithic hunter-fisher people, represented largely by flintwork found mainly in ancient beaches in the historic counties of Antrim, Down, Louth, and Dublin. These artifacts were named Larnian, after Larne, Northern Ireland, the site where they were first found; dates from 6000 BCE onward were assigned to them. Archaeological work since World War II, however, casts considerable doubt on the antiquity and affinities of the people who were responsible for the Larnian industry; association with Neolithic remains suggests that they should be considered not as a Mesolithic people but rather as groups contemporary with the Neolithic farmers. The Larnian could then be interpreted as a specialized aspect of contemporary Neolithic culture. Lake and riverside finds, especially along the River Bann, show a comparable tradition. A single carbon-14 date of 5725 ± 110 BCE from Toome Bay, north of Lough Neagh, for woodworking and flint has been cited in support of a Mesolithic phase in Ireland, but such a single date cannot be considered reliable.

NEOLITHIC PERIOD

The general pattern of carbon-14 date determinations suggests that the Neolithic Period (New Stone Age) in Ireland began about 3000 BCE. As in Britain, the most widespread evidence of early farming communities is long-barrow burial.

Neolithic burial mound, Newgrange, County Meath. Brian Morrison/Tourism Ireland

The main Irish long-barrow series consists of megalithic tombs called court tombs because an oval or semicircular open space, or court, inset into the end of the long barrow precedes the burial chamber. There are more than 300 of these court tombs. They occur in the northern half of Ireland, and the distribution is bounded on the south by the lowlands of the central plain. Timber-built rectangular houses belonging to the court tomb builders have been discovered at Ballynagilly, County Tyrone, and at Ballyglass, County Mayo. The court tombs are intimately related to the British long-barrow series of the Severn-Cotswold and chalk regions and probably derive from more or less common prototypes in northwestern France.

In Ireland a second type of megalithic long barrow—the so-called portal tomb, of which there are more than 150 examples—developed from the court tomb. They spread across the court tomb area in the northern half of Ireland and extend into Leinster and Waterford and also to western Wales and Cornwall.

Another notable feature of the Irish Neolithic is the passage tomb. This megalithic tomb, unlike the long-barrow types, is set in a round mound, sited usually on a hilltop and grouped in cemeteries. The rich grave goods of these tombs include beads, pendants, and bone pins. Many of the stones of the tombs are elaborately decorated with engraved designs. The main axis of the distribution lies along a series of great cemeteries from the River Boyne to Sligo (Boyne and Loughcrew in County Meath, Carrowkeel and Carrowmore in County Sligo). Smaller groups and single

Poulnabrone Dolmen, a prehistoric megalithic tomb in County Clare. Holger Leue/Tourism Ireland

tombs occur largely in the northern half of the country and in Leinster. A specialized group of later—indeed, advanced Bronze Age—date near Tramore, County Waterford, is quite similar to a large group on the Isles of Scilly and Cornwall. The great Irish passage tombs include some of the most magnificent megalithic tombs in all of Europe—for example, Newgrange and Knowth in Meath. While the passage tombs represent the arrival of the megalithic tradition in its fullest and most sophisticated form, the exact relation between the builders of these tombs and the more or less contemporary long-barrow builders is not clear. The passage tombs suggest rather more clearly integrated communities than do the long barrows.

To the final stage of the Neolithic probably belong the rich house sites of both rectangular and circular form at Lough Gur, County Limerick. The pottery shows a strong connection with the tradition of the long barrow (court tomb and portal tomb).

BRONZE AGE

Two great incursions establish the early Bronze Age in Ireland. One, represented by approximately 400 megalithic tombs of the wedge tomb variety, is associated with Beaker pottery. This group is dominant in the western half of the country. Similar tombs also associated with Beaker finds are common in the French region of Brittany, and the origin of the Irish series is clearly from this region. In Ireland the distribution indicates that these tomb builders sought well-drained grazing land, such as the Burren limestones in Clare, and also copper deposits, such as those on the Cork-Kerry coast and around the Silvermines area of Tipperary.

In contrast, in the eastern half of the country a people in the single-burial tradition dominate. Their burial modes and distinctive pottery, known as food vessels, have strong roots in the Beaker tradition that dominates in many areas of western Europe. They may have reached Ireland via Britain from the lowland areas around the Rhine or farther north.

Throughout the early Bronze Age Ireland had a flourishing metal industry, and bronze, copper, and gold objects were exported widely to Britain and the Continent. In the middle Bronze Age (about 1500 BCE) new influences brought urn burial into eastern Ireland. From about 1200 BCE elements of a late Bronze Age appear, and by about 800 BCE a great late Bronze Age industry was established. A considerable wealth of bronze and gold is present, an example of which is the great Clare gold hoard. Nordic connections have been noted in much of this metalwork.

IRON AGE

The period of the transition from the Bronze Age to the Iron Age in Ireland is fraught with uncertainties. The problem of identifying archaeological remains with language grouping is notoriously difficult, but it seems likely that the principal Celtic arrivals occurred in the Iron Age. Irish sagas, which probably reflect the pagan Irish Iron Age, reveal conditions in many respects similar to the descriptions of the ancient Classical authors, such as Poseidonius and Julius Caesar. The Celts were an Indo-European group who are thought to have originated in the 2nd millennium BCE, probably in east-central Europe. They were among the earliest to develop an Iron Age culture, as has been found at Hallstatt, Austria (c. 700 BCE). Although there is little sign of Hallstatt-like culture in Ireland, the later La Tène culture (which may date in Ireland from 300 BCE or earlier) is represented in metalwork and some stone sculpture, mainly in the northern half of the country. Connections with northern England are apparent. Hill fort building seems also characteristic of the Iron Age.

EARLY CELTIC IRELAND

Politically, Ireland was organized into a number of petty kingdoms, or clans (*tuatha*), each of which was quite independent under its elected king. Groups of *tuatha* tended to combine, but the king who claimed overlordship in each group had a primacy of honour rather than of jurisdiction. Not until the 10th century CE was there a king of all Ireland (*árd rí Éireann*). A division of the country into five groups of *tuatha*, known as the Five Fifths (Cuíg Cuígí), occurred about the beginning of the Christian era. These were Ulster (Ulaidh), Meath (Midhe), Leinster (Laighin), Munster (Mumhain), and Connaught (Connacht).

Surrounding a king was an aristocracy (*airi aicme*, the upper class), whose land and property rights were clearly defined by law and whose main wealth was in cattle. Greater landowners were supported by *céilí*, or clients. These and other grades of society, minutely classified and described by legal writers, tilled the soil and tended the cattle. Individual families were the real units of society and collectively exercised powers of ownership over their farms and territory. At law the family (*fine*) did not merely act corporately but was, by one of the oldest customs, held responsible for the observance of the law by its kindred, serfs, and slaves.

RURAL ECONOMY AND LIVING CONDITIONS

There were no urban centres, and the economic basis of society was cattle rearing and agriculture. The principal crops were wheat, barley, oats, flax, and hay. The land was tilled with plows drawn by oxen. Sheep appear to have been bred principally for their wool, and the only animal reared specifically for slaughter was the pig. Fishing, hunting, fowling, and trapping provided additional food. The transport of goods over land was by packhorse, for wheeled vehicles appear to have been few. Sea transport was by curragh, a wicker-framed boat covered with hides; the normal freshwater craft was the dugout.

The dwellings of the period were built by the post-and-wattle technique, and some were situated within the protected sites archaeologists call ring forts. Excavations have shown that some of these may have existed even in the Bronze Age and that they remained a normal place of habitation until medieval times. Advantage was also taken of the relative security of islands in rivers or lakes as dwelling places; and artificial islands, called crannogs, were also extensively made.

The Irish laws point to a large development of rural industry in the period in which they were first written down, shortly before the Norse invasions beginning at the end of the 8th century. They deal minutely not only with the management of land and animal rearing but also with innumerable further details of husbandry, including milling, dyeing, dairying, malting, meat curing, and spinning and weaving. Wool was spun with a wooden spindle weighted with a whorl of bone or stone, and it was woven on a loom. The outer garment worn by both men and women was a large woolen cloak (*brat*), fastened on the shoulder or breast with a pin or brooch. The inner garment was a long linen tunic (*léine*), girded at the waist with a belt. Shoes of rawhide or tanned leather were worn, at least by the upper classes and the higher professional ranks. A large amount of metalwork reveals the adaptation by Irish craftsmen of many techniques originating in Britain or on the European continent. An instinct for design, added to the skillful

TARA BROOCH

Found on the seashore at Bettystown, south of Drogheda, and now preserved in the National Museum of Ireland, Dublin, the Tara brooch, which probably dates from the 8th century, is of white bronze and consists of a large circle with about half of the centre empty and the other half filled in with sunken panels ornamented in extremely delicate filigree.

On the reverse side there is elaborate chasing consisting mainly of Celtic spiral forms and delicate interlaced patterns. A pin thrust through the brooch attached the whole to the garment; it is of exaggerated length with an elaborately decorated head. The brooch was probably worn on the shoulder with the pin pointing upward.

The gold, enamel, and amber Tara brooch, kept at the National Museum of Ireland, Dublin, attests to the fine craftsmanship of 8th-century Celtic artisans. The Bridgeman Art Library/Getty Images

use of these techniques, enabled them to produce many superb objects, of which the Tara brooch, dating from about the mid-8th century, is an outstanding example. The chief musical instrument of the period was the harp.

EARLY POLITICAL HISTORY

The documentary history of Ireland begins only in the 7th century, which saw the production in both Latin and Irish of sufficiently rich and numerous records of all sorts. For events before that time, historians rely on literary sources such as the sagas, many of whose characters may represent only poetic imagination and in which the social or political circumstances portrayed reflect the fantasies of their authors rather than historical reality. Nevertheless, the traditions seem to indicate, during the early centuries CE, a process of political cohesion in Ireland through which the *tuatha* ultimately became grouped into the Five Fifths. Among these, Ulster seems at first to have been dominant; but, by the time Niall of the Nine Hostages died early in the 5th century, hegemony had passed to his midland kingdom of Meath, which was then temporarily associated with Connaught. In the 6th century, descendants of Niall, ruling at Tara in northern Leinster, were claiming to be overkings of three provinces, Ulster, Connaught, and Meath. Later they claimed to be kings of all of Ireland, although their power rarely extended over Munster or the greater part of Leinster. Two branches of Niall's descendants, the Cenél nEogain, of the northern Uí Néill, and the Clan Cholmáin, of the southern Uí Néill, alternated as kings of Ireland from 734 to 1002, a fact that suggests a formal arrangement

TARA

A low hill (about 507 feet [154 m] in elevation) in County Meath, Tara (Irish: "Place of Assembly") occupies an important place in Irish legend and history. The earliest local remains consist of a small passage grave (c. 2100 BCE) known as Dumha na nGiall ("Mound of the Hostages"). Numerous Bronze Age burials were found in the earth mound, which lies just inside the perimeter of a vast oval enclosure called Ráth na Ríógh ("Fortress of the Kings"). Near the centre of this are two conjoined earthworks: Forradh ("Royal Seat") and Teach Cormaic ("Cormac's House"). On the latter is a pillar stone, often thought to be the inauguration stone of the kings of Tara. The other principal sites are a large ring fort, two circular enclosures, and a great rectangular earthwork 750 feet (230 m) long, which is usually identified as the banqueting hall. The Rath of the Synods is a ritual site that underwent four enlargements between the 1st and the 4th centuries.

The main earthworks on the hill probably date to the first five centuries of the Christian era, when Tara was the seat of a dynasty of Ui Néill kings, who appear to have abandoned it in the 6th century.

between the two septs (i.e., descendants of a common ancestor). Inevitably, claims to a high kingship came to be contested by the rulers of Munster, who, from their capital at Cashel, had gradually increased their strength, depriving Connaught of the region that later became County Clare. But not until the reign of Brian Boru in the 11th century was Munster sufficiently strong to secure a real high kingship over all of Ireland.

IRISH RAIDS AND MIGRATIONS

Latin writings from about the mid-3rd century make frequent reference to raiding expeditions carried out by the Irish, who were now given the new name Scoti rather than the older one Hiberni. In the second half of the 4th century, when Roman power in Britain was beginning to crumble seriously, the raids became incessant, and settlements were made along the west coast of Britain and extensively in Wales and Scotland. From the early 5th century the rulers of Dalriada in northern Antrim extended their power over the Irish already settled in Argyll and the neighbouring islands. Ultimately the Scottish kingdom of Dalriada became separated from the Irish; in the 9th century, when it overcame the Picts, it gave its name, Scotland, to the whole area.

EARLY CHRISTIANITY

Little is known of the first impact of Christianity on Ireland. Traditions in the south and southeast refer to early saints who allegedly preceded St. Patrick, and their missions may well have come through trading relations with the Roman Empire. The earliest firm date is 431 CE, when St. Germanus, bishop of Auxerre in Gaul, proposed, with the approval of Pope Celestine I, to send a certain Palladius to "the Scots believing in Christ." Subsequent missionary history in Ireland is dominated by the figure of St. Patrick, whose 7th-century biographers, Tirechán

DALRIADA

From about the 5th century CE the Gaelic kingdom of Dalriada (Irish: Dál Riada or Riatathat) extended on both sides of the North Channel and composed the northern part of the present County Antrim, Northern Ireland, and part of the Inner Hebrides and Argyll, in Scotland. In earlier times, Argyll had received extensive immigration from the Irish (known as Scoti until the 12th century) of northern Ireland and had become an Irish (i.e., "Scottish") area. In c. 500, the ruling family of Irish Dalriada crossed into Scottish Dalriada and made Dunadd and Dunolly its chief strongholds. Irish Dalriada gradually declined; and after the Viking invasions early in the 9th century, it lost all political identity. Heavy onslaughts from the Picts checked the Dalriada of the Scottish mainland. In the mid-9th century its king Kenneth I MacAlpin brought the Picts and Scoti permanently together, and thereafter the whole country was known as Scotland.

and Muirchú, credited him with converting all the Irish to Christianity and won for him the status of national apostle.

A 9th-century record, the Book of Armagh, includes a work by Patrick himself, the *Confessio* ("Confession," a reply to charges made by British ecclesiastics), in which he describes his life at a Roman villa in Britain, his capture by Irish raiders, and his seven years of slavery in Ireland. Recovering his freedom, he claimed he was educated and ordained into the priesthood and eventually managed to be sent as a missionary to Ireland. He concentrated on the north and west of the country, achieving remarkable success; he did not himself claim to have converted all of Ireland. Confusion exists regarding the chronology of Patrick's life, and it is seriously contended that tradition came to merge the experience of two men, the continental Palladius and the Patrick of the *Confessio*. No sufficient evidence supports the traditional date (432) for the beginning of Patrick's mission; of the rival dates (461/462 and 492/493) given for his death in annals and biographies, the latter is now preferred.

IRISH MONASTICISM

Although monks and monasteries were to be found in Ireland at the time of Patrick, their place was then altogether secondary. But in the course of the 6th and 7th centuries a comprehensive monastic system developed in Ireland, partly through the influence of Celtic monasteries in Britain, such as Candida Casa at Whithorn in Galloway and Llangarvan in Wales. Early attempts to organize the Irish church on the usual Roman system—by which each bishop and his clergy exercised exclusive jurisdiction within a diocese—seem to have given way to one in which groups of Christian settlements were loosely linked together, usually under the auspices of some one or other of the great saints. Careful study of the lives of the early saints reveals the manner in which their reputations developed in proportion to the power of the political dynasties that became connected with them.

By the end of the 6th century, enthusiasm for Christianity was leading Irishmen to devote themselves to a most austere existence as monks, as hermits, and as missionaries to pagan tribes in Scotland and the north of England and in a great area of west-central Europe, particularly between the Rhine, Loire, and Rhône rivers. St. Columba's foundation (c. 563) of the monastery of Iona off the northwest Scottish coast provided the best-known base for the Celtic Christianization of Scotland; and its offshoot, Lindisfarne (Holy Island), lying off the coast of the Anglo-Saxon kingdom of Northumbria, was responsible for the conversion of that area. Of the continental missionaries, the best-known is St. Columban (c. 543–615), whose monastic foundations at Luxeuil near Annegray in the Vosges and at Bobbio in northern Italy became important centres of learning. Columban, however, by his individualism and austere puritanism, came into conflict not only with the Merovingian rulers of Gaul but also with the local ecclesiastical administration; his limitations exemplify those of the Irish monastic system as a whole and explain why, in the end, it was supplanted by the ordinary administrative system of the church.

LEARNING AND ART

Both at home and abroad the saints were succeeded by scholars, whose work in sacred and classical studies and particularly in elaborating an Irish Christian mythology and literature was to have profound effects on the Irish language and was to be a major factor in its survival. The Irish monasteries—with those in Clonmacnoise and Clonard among the most famous—became notable centres of learning. Christianity brought Latin to Ireland, and the writings of both the Church Fathers and Classical authors were read and studied. Irish scribes produced manuscripts written in the clear hand known as Insular; this usage spread from Ireland to Anglo-Saxon England and to Irish monasteries on the European continent. Initial letters in the manuscripts were illuminated, usually with intricate ribbon and zoomorphic designs. The most famous of the Irish manuscripts is the Book of Kells, a copy of the four Gospels probably dating from the late 8th to the early 9th century. The earliest surviving illuminated manuscript, the Book of Durrow, was probably made about a century earlier.

The adoption of Christianity made it necessary to relate the chronology of Irish tradition, history, and genealogies to the events recorded in the Bible. The Book of Invasions (*Leabhar Gabhála*), in which Irish history was linked with events in the Hebrew Bible was a notable example of this process. In this way Latin civilization in Ireland became linked to the Gaelic, and the association became closer under the impact of the Viking wars. Gradually the Latin products of the Christian schools became replaced by Irish works; for example, Latin lives of the saints are almost always earlier in date than those written in Irish. Recurring bouts of puritanism and reforming movements in the church tended to remove secular literature from monastic control; ultimately there developed a class of professional families who were its custodians from the 12th to the 17th century. The medieval secular writers, employing a degenerate form of Old Irish usually known as Middle Irish, were responsible for a large proportion of Irish literary achievement; their historical works, the annals, and the great genealogies, supplemented by the law collections, have enabled historians to reconstruct early Irish social history.

THE NORSE INVASIONS AND THEIR AFTERMATH

The first appearance of the Norsemen on the Irish coast is recorded in 795. Thereafter the Norsemen made frequent plundering raids, sometimes far inland. In 838 they seized and fortified two ports, Annagassan and Dublin, and in the 840s they undertook a series of large-scale invasions in

An illumination from the Book of Kells shows Saint Matthew. Photos.com/Thinkstock

the north of the country. These invaders were driven out by Aed Finnliath, high king from 862 to 879, but meanwhile the Norse rulers of Dublin were reaching the zenith of their power. They took Waterford in 914 and Limerick in 920. Gradually, without quite abandoning piracy, the Vikings became traders in close association with the Irish, and their commercial towns became a new element in the life of the country. The decline of Norse power in the south began when they lost Limerick in 968 and was finally effected when the Scandinavian allies of the king of Dublin were defeated by High King Brian Boru at the Battle of Clontarf in 1014.

Although the Battle of Clontarf removed the prospect of Norse domination, it brought a period of political unsettlement. High kings ruled in Ireland but almost always "with opposition," meaning they were not acknowledged by a minority of provincial kings. The Viking invasions had, in fact, shown the strength and the weakness of the Irish position. The fact that power had been preserved at a local level in Ireland enabled a maximum of resistance to be made; and, although the invaders established maritime strongholds, they never achieved any domination comparable to their control of eastern England or northwestern France. After Clontarf they remained largely in control of Ireland's commerce but came increasingly under the influence of neighbouring Irish kings.

In the 11th and 12th centuries the ecclesiastical reform movement of western Europe was extended into Ireland. As the kings of Munster and Connaught, along with those of Leinster and Ulster, each struggled to secure the dominant position that had once been held by Brian Boru, they came to realize the value to them of alliance with the forces of church reform. Thus, with the aid of provincial rulers, the reformers established in Ireland a system of dioceses whose

CLONMACNOISE

Clonmacnoise (Irish: Cluain Mhic Nóis) was the earliest and foremost Irish monastic city after the foundation of an abbey there by St. Ciaran about 545. It lies on the left bank of the River Shannon in County Offaly, about 70 miles (110 km) west of Dublin. It had become an important centre of learning by the 9th century, and several books of annals were compiled there. The cathedral, or Great Church, was founded about 900 and rebuilt in the 14th century. Other churches are those dedicated to Finian (Finghin), Conor (Connor), St. Ciaran, Kelly, Ri, and Dowling (Doolin). Clonmacnoise became a bishopric, and in 1568 the diocese was merged with that of Meath. The ruins of the churches, known as the Seven Churches of Clonmacnoise, and two 12th-century towers still survive and are protected as part of a national monument. An annual pilgrimage to Clonmacnoise is held on September 9, the feast of St. Ciaran. Attesting to the city's historic and religious importance, Pope John Paul II visited the town during his trip to Ireland in 1979.

boundaries were coterminous with those of the chief petty kingdoms. At the head of this hierarchy was established the archbishopric of Armagh, in association with the province of Ulster dominated by the royal family of Uí Néill. But the victory of the reformers was not complete, for the parochial system was not introduced until after the Anglo-Norman invasion. Moreover, the reformers sought to influence Irish conduct as well as church organization. The enormities of Irish moral behaviour were colourfully described by St. Bernard of Clairvaux in his life of his contemporary St. Malachy, the reforming bishop who introduced the Cistercian monks into Ireland. The reforming popes Adrian IV and Alexander III encouraged Henry II's invasion of Ireland, believing that it would further church reform in that country. In a remarkable account of the conquest, Giraldus Cambrensis (Gerald of Wales) provided a lurid description of the archaic Irish civilization that the invaders encountered. The recognition of Henry II as lord of Ireland and the linking of the church to a foreign administration terminated the independence of Gaelic Ireland and reduced the country to a position of subordination for centuries to come.

Dromoland Castle, County Clare. Tourism Ireland

FIRST CENTURIES OF ENGLISH RULE (*c.* 1166–*c.* 1600)

Before the arrival of Henry II in Ireland (October 1171), Anglo-Norman adventurers—including Richard de Clare, earl of Pembroke, subsequently known as Strongbow, invited by Dermot MacMurrough, a king of Leinster who had been expelled by the high king, Roderic O'Connor—had conquered a substantial part of eastern Ireland, including the kingdom of Leinster, the towns of Waterford, Wexford, and Dublin, and part of the kingdom of Meath. Partly to avert any chance of Ireland's becoming a rival Norman state, Henry took action to impose his rule there. He granted Leinster to de Clare and Meath to Hugh de Lacy, who had gone to Ireland in the

Administrative units of late medieval Ireland.

except in the northwest, agreed to recognize his supremacy, Henry was obliged to acquiesce in the establishment of new Norman lordships in Ulster under John de Courci and in Munster under de Cogan, de Braose, and others. By the Treaty of Windsor (1175), O'Connor, the high king, accepted Henry as his overlord and restyled himself as only the king of Connaught. But he was permitted to exercise some vague authority over the other Irish kings and was charged with collecting from them tribute to be paid to Henry. This arrangement was unsuccessful, for thereafter O'Connor encountered opposition even in his own province, and he was ultimately obliged to abdicate.

King John, who visited Ireland in 1210, established there a civil government independent of the feudal lords, and during the 13th century it became more fully organized. An Irish exchequer had been set up in 1200, and a chancery followed in 1232. The country was divided into counties for administrative purposes, English law was introduced, and serious attempts were made to reduce the feudal liberties of the Anglo-Norman baronage. (Counties were civil administration districts, whereas liberties were lands held in the personal control of aristocratic families and the church.) The development of the Irish Parliament paralleled that of its English counterpart; in 1297 the peers and prelates were joined by

king's army, but he kept the chief towns in his own hands, exacted forms of submission from the Irish kings, and secured from a church synod recognition of his overlordship. During subsequent years the Anglo-Norman sphere in Ireland was extended, and, while all the Irish kings,

representatives of counties, and in 1300 the towns also sent members. But these represented the Anglo-Irish only, as the native Irish—to some extent resurgent in Ulster under the O'Neills and O'Donnells and in southwest Munster under the MacCarthys—went unrepresented.

THE 14TH AND 15TH CENTURIES

A brief threat to English control of Ireland, made by Edward Bruce, brother of King Robert I of Scotland, ended when Bruce was killed in battle at Faughart near Dundalk (1318). English control was reasserted and strengthened by the creation of three new Anglo-Irish earldoms: Kildare, given to the head of the Leinster Fitzgeralds; Desmond, given to the head of the Munster Fitzgeralds; and Ormonde, given to the head of the Butlers, who held lands around Tipperary. The increased power and lands of the Anglo-Irish brought about an inevitable reaction, and during the remainder of the 14th century there was a remarkable revival of Irish political power, which was matched by a flowering of Irish language, law, and civilization. The Gaels recovered large parts of Ulster, the midlands, Connaught, and Leinster, while the Anglo-Irish became increasingly Irish, marrying Irish women and often adopting Gaelic customs.

RICHARD FITZGILBERT, 2ND EARL OF PEMBROKE

Richard FitzGilbert, 2nd earl of Pembroke (born *c.* 1130—died April 20, 1176, Dublin), initiated the opening phase of the English conquest of Ireland with his invasion in 1170. Better known later as Richard Strongbow (and also called Richard De Clare), he was the son of Gilbert FitzGilbert, 1st earl of Pembroke, and he succeeded to his father's estates in southern Wales in 1148/49. Pembroke had evidently lost these lands by 1168; it was probably in that year that he agreed to aid Dermot MacMurrough, king of Leinster, who had been expelled from his kingdom by Roderic (Rory O'Connor), high king of Ireland. King Henry II of England (reigned 1154–89) granted Pembroke permission to invade Ireland, and on August 23, 1170, the earl landed near Waterford. Waterford and Dublin quickly fell to the Normans. After the death of MacMurrough in May 1171, Pembroke was besieged in Dublin by Roderic, but in September his forces broke out and routed Roderic's army. In order to prevent Pembroke from setting himself up as an independent ruler, Henry II had him acknowledge royal authority over his conquests in Leinster. Pembroke helped the king suppress a rebellion in Normandy in 1173–74, and in return Henry granted him custody of Wexford, Waterford, and Dublin. By the time Pembroke died, all Ireland had been committed to his care, but within Ireland his supremacy was recognized only in Leinster.

His son Gilbert de Striguil (or Strigoil) died unmarried, certainly before 1189, and as a minor was never styled earl. The earldom passed with Richard's daughter Isabel (d. 1220) to her husband William Marshal, the 1st Earl of Pembroke in the Marshal line.

The English government, which was always to some extent opposed by the Anglo-Norman aristocracy because of its aim to curtail feudal privileges, made an effort to restore control but achieved little more than a definition of the status quo. Edward III's son, Lionel, duke of Clarence, as viceroy from 1361 to 1367 passed in the Irish Parliament the Statute of Kilkenny (1366), which listed the "obedient" (English-controlled) lands as Louth, Meath, Trim, Dublin, Carlow, Kildare, Kilkenny, Wexford, Waterford, and Tipperary. Intermarriage or alliances with the Irish were forbidden. The independent Irish outside the Pale (the area of English control) were regarded as enemies and were assumed to possess their lands only by usurpation. In practice they were feared, and their attacks were often bought off by regular payments. Visits by King Richard II in 1394–95 and 1399 achieved nothing. During the first half of the 15th century, Ireland was, in effect, ruled by the three great earls—of Desmond, Ormonde, and Kildare—who combined to dominate the Dublin government. Desmond had sway in the counties of Limerick, Cork, Kerry, and Waterford; Ormonde in Tipperary and Kilkenny; and Kildare in Leinster. Although both the Gaels and the Anglo-Irish had supported the Yorkist side in the Wars of the Roses, the Yorkist king Edward IV found them no less easy to subjugate than had his Lancastrian predecessors. Succeeding in 1468 in bringing about the attainder and execution for treason of Thomas, earl of Desmond, Edward was nevertheless obliged to yield to aristocratic power in Ireland. The earls of Kildare, who thereafter bore the title of lords deputy (for the English princes who were lords lieutenant), were in effect the actual rulers of Ireland until well into the 16th century.

THE KILDARE ASCENDANCY

The substitution (1485) of Tudor for Yorkist rule in England had no apparent effect in Ireland, where the ascendancy of the Fitzgerald earls of Kildare, established when Thomas, 7th earl, was created lord deputy in 1471, had passed (1477) to his son Garret Mór (Great Gerald). The formality of royal power was preserved by appointing an absentee lieutenant, for whom Kildare acted as deputy. In practice, Kildare exercised real power through dynastic alliances with the chief Gaelic and Anglo-Irish lords. Opposition to Kildare was negligible even when he gave support (1487) to Lambert Simnel, a pretender to the English throne. After the advent of a more dangerous pretender, Perkin Warbeck, in 1494 it was decided to remove Kildare and rule through an Englishman, Sir Edward Poynings. Poynings subdued Kildare, but he could not reconquer the northern Gaelic Irish. At Drogheda (1494–95) he induced Parliament to pass an act that came to be known as "Poynings's Law," which subjected the meetings and legislative drafts of the Irish Parliament to the control of the English king and council. But

Poynings's administrative expenses were too great, and Henry VII decided in 1496 to restore Kildare.

On Kildare's death (1513) the deputyship passed to his son Garret Óg (Young Gerald), 9th earl of Kildare, who continued, though less impressively, to dominate the country. But James, 10th earl of Desmond, intrigued with the Holy Roman emperor Charles V; and Henry VIII became convinced that Kildare had lost the power to control Ireland in the interests of the English crown. Therefore, when Henry's divorce of Catherine of Aragon in 1533 made the danger of imperial intervention particularly acute, the king dismissed Kildare (1534). Thereafter there were no Irish-born viceroys for more than a century.

THE REFORMATION PERIOD

Rumours that Kildare had been executed precipitated the rebellion of his son, Thomas Fitzgerald, Lord Offaly, called Silken Thomas. The rebellion facilitated the transition to the new system. Silken Thomas had opposed Henry VIII's breach with Rome; his rebellion failed and he was executed in 1537. This caused a revival of the power of the Butlers of Ormonde; Piers Butler, earl of Ossory, helped to secure the enactment of royal (instead of papal) ecclesiastical supremacy by the Dublin Parliament of 1536–37. As a further step in shedding papal authority,

The English plantation of Ireland in the 16th and 17th centuries.

in 1541 a complaisant Parliament recognized Henry VIII as king of Ireland (his predecessors had held the title of lord of Ireland). Confiscation of monastic property, as well as the lands of the rebels, met most of the costs of the expanded administration. This loss of land inevitably drove the religious orders and the Anglo-Irish into the arms of the Gaelic Irish, thus weakening the old ethnic rivalries of medieval Ireland.

Sir Anthony Saint Leger, lord deputy in 1540–48 and again in 1550–56, then began a conciliatory policy by which outstanding lords were persuaded to renounce the pope and recognize the king's ecclesiastical supremacy in order to gain new titles and grants of lands. This policy, however, required a steady series of efficient governors and disciplined administrators; in fact, neither in Tudor nor in Stuart times did the English succeed in converting elective chiefs into hereditary nobles holding offices delegated by the crown.

Moreover, even those who had recently submitted were often condemned for religious conservatism and deprived of their lands. Saint Leger's personal success was all the more remarkable because the first Jesuit mission to Ireland arrived in the north in 1542.

Under Edward VI (1547–53) the Dublin authorities carried out a forward policy in religion as well as in politics, but Protestantism got no support except from English officials. The official restoration of Roman Catholicism under Queen Mary (1553–58) revealed the strength of resentment in Ireland against Protestantism. As in England, the papal jurisdiction was restored, but otherwise the Tudor regulations of authority were observed. The pope was induced to recognize the conversion of the Tudor Irish lordship into a kingdom. Finally Mary gave statutory approval for the plantation (or resettlement of Irish lands by Englishmen) of Leix, Offaly, and other

THOMAS FITZGERALD, 10TH EARL OF KILDARE

When his father, the Irish lord deputy Gerald, 9th Earl of Kildare, was called to London in February 1534 to answer charges of disloyalty, Thomas Fitzgerald, 10th earl of Kildare (born 1513, London—died February 3, 1537, London), was left in charge of Ireland. Rumour that his father had been executed caused Fitzgerald to renounce allegiance to Henry VIII and assert allegiance to papal authority in June 1534. (His father was not to die until the following September—of natural causes.) Fitzgerald seized Dublin, and his partisans murdered Archbishop John Alen. Henry had already appointed Sir William Skeffington as lord deputy. Skeffington recaptured Dublin and in March 1535 stormed Fitzgerald's stronghold, Maynooth Castle. Recognizing that he would not receive the aid he had expected from Spain or Scotland, Fitzgerald (who was known as Silken Thomas) surrendered in August 1535. After Ireland had been completely pacified 18 months later, he and his five uncles were hanged for treason.

Irish lordships of the central plain. Her viceroy was Thomas Radcliffe, earl of Sussex, lord deputy (1556–59), who was soon, as lord lieutenant (1559–66) for Elizabeth I, to restore the state's authority over the church.

IRELAND UNDER ELIZABETH I

The Acts of Supremacy and Uniformity, which enforced the Anglican church settlement, were passed in Ireland in 1560, but fear of driving the inhabitants of the Pale into alliance with the Gaelic Irish (and perhaps with the Spanish) made the government lenient in enforcing the terms of the acts. Political affairs continued to preoccupy the administrators, so that the new Protestant church was unequipped to resist the forces of the Counter-Reformation. This was inevitable in an Ireland only superficially conformed to royal obedience, but the seriousness of the situation was shown by the three great rebellions of the reign, those of Shane O'Neill (1559), of the Fitzgeralds of Desmond (1568–83), and of O'Neill (Tyrone) and O'Donnell (1594–1603).

THE SHANE O'NEILL REBELLION

The first of these rebellions, that of Shane O'Neill, fully exposed the weakness and later the folly of the government. O'Neill's father, Conn the Lame (Conn Bacach), who as the "O'Neill" was head of a whole network of clans, had been made earl of Tyrone in 1541, and the succession rights of his illegitimate son Feardorchadh (Matthew) were recognized. Shane, younger but the eldest legitimate son, was elected O'Neill on his father's death in 1559, and soon afterward Feardorchadh was killed. O'Neill then battled against the Dublin government, demanding recognition according to the laws of primogeniture, and he insisted that neither of Feardorchadh's sons, Brian and Hugh, had claims to the earldom. Elizabeth invited O'Neill to London to negotiate, but the opportunity for a statesmanlike settlement was lost. O'Neill was to be "captain of Tyrone" and was encouraged to expel from Antrim the MacDonnell (MacDonald or MacConnell) migrants from Scotland. Returning to Ireland in May 1562, O'Neill routed the MacDonnells, as well as the loyal O'Donnells of the northwest, and attempted to secure support from Scotland and France. Eventually the government was saved from a serious situation only through the defeat of O'Neill by the O'Donnells and his murder in 1567 by the MacDonnells.

The lands of the O'Neills and even of loyal Gaelic lords were declared forfeit in 1569, and, in a wave of enthusiasm for colonization, various questionable adventurers were permitted to attempt substantial plantations in Munster, Leinster, and Ulster. The folly of this policy was seen when the government, despite its having declared the position of "O'Neill" extinguished, allowed the O'Neills to elect Shane's cousin Turlough Luineach as their chief. Butlers and Munster Fitzgeralds also combined forcibly to resist the plantations. The only gleam of statesmanship shown in these years by Henry Sidney, lord deputy (1565–71, 1575–78), was that he managed to avoid a major combination against the government's religious policy. The Butlers were induced to submit, the planters were given only limited support, and a head-on collision with Turlough Luineach was averted. When the Ulster plantation plans could not be carried out against Irish resistance, the queen wisely decided that they should be dropped. The pardon of the Butlers pacified Leinster, and, although in Munster the earl of Desmond's cousin James Fitzgerald, called "Fitzmaurice," attempted to make the war one of religion, he, too, was eventually pardoned.

THE DESMOND REBELLION

Despite his pardon, Fitzmaurice fled to the European continent in 1575, returning to Ireland in 1579 with papal approval for a Roman Catholic crusade against Queen Elizabeth. Although neither France nor Spain supported the crusade and Fitzmaurice was surprised and killed in August 1579, the government was extremely apprehensive. Gerald Fitzgerald, 14th earl of Desmond, then assumed direction of the enterprise. As a military commander he was wholly deficient, and his mediocrity may well have kept outstanding figures in the north and west out of the movement. The rebels were defeated, and in November 1580 a force of Italians and Spaniards was massacred at Dún an Óir ("Golden Fort"), Smerwick Harbour, County Kerry.

The end of the Desmond rebellion gave the government the opportunity to confiscate more than 300,000 acres (100,000 hectares) in Munster and initiate more stringent proceedings against Roman Catholics. But the plantation was not a success. A more statesman-like attitude was displayed in regard to Connaught land titles. When Sir John Perrot was lord deputy (1584–88), a number of agreements were made with individual landowners and chieftains by which their titles were officially recognized in return for regular fixed payments. This was a step in the process of converting a great part of the country to English tenures. Perrot was less successful in handling the 1585–86 Parliament, in which the government's anti-Catholic program was defeated by the opposition.

THE TYRONE REBELLION

The origins of the third rebellion, the O'Neill (Tyrone) war, remain in doubt. Both Hugh Roe O'Donnell and Hugh O'Neill (younger son of Feardorchadh), for whom the earldom of Tyrone had been revived in 1585 and who had been elected O'Neill on Turlough Luineach's death in 1595, certainly resented the extension of the royal administration, but the religious issue was probably more important. For a generation, exiled Roman Catholics had been trained as missionaries in the continental colleges of the Counter-Reformation, and the majority of those who returned to Ireland concluded that Catholicism could survive there only if Elizabeth were defeated. The outbreak of hostilities in Ulster in 1594 was at first confined to the northwest, where O'Donnell and Maguire, lord of Fermanagh, tried to drive out the English troops. The intervention of Hugh O'Neill was expected, if not inevitable. His participation with his brother-in-law O'Donnell proved decisive in the north and west, and the English were defeated both in Ulster and in Connaught. A more intimidating combination thus threatened Dublin than even in Shane O'Neill's time. Even in the Pale, arbitrary exactions and exclusion from offices won Hugh much sympathy, and it was said that he knew of Dublin Castle decisions before they were known in the city. Resentful of O'Neill's alleged ingratitude, Elizabeth

HUGH O'NEILL, 2ND EARL OF TYRONE

From 1595 to 1603, Hugh O'Neill, 2nd earl of Tyrone (born c. 1540—died July 20, 1616, Rome, Papal States [Italy]), led an unsuccessful Roman Catholic uprising against English rule in Ireland. The defeat of O'Neill and the conquest of his province of Ulster was the final step in the subjugation of Ireland by the English.

Although born into the powerful O'Neill family of Ulster, Hugh grew up in London. In 1568 he returned to Ireland and assumed his grandfather's title of Earl of Tyrone. By cooperating with the government of Queen Elizabeth I, he established his base of power, and in 1593 he replaced Turlough Luineach O'Neill as chieftain of the O'Neills. Skirmishes between Tyrone's forces and the English in 1595 were followed by three years of fruitless negotiations between the two sides.

In 1598 Tyrone (who was known as the Great Earl) reopened hostilities. His victory (August 14) over the English in the Battle of the Yellow Ford on the Blackwater River, Ulster—the most serious defeat sustained by the English in the Irish wars—sparked a general revolt throughout the country. Pope Clement VIII lent moral support to Tyrone's cause, and, in September 1601, 4,000 Spanish troops arrived at Kinsale, Munster, to assist the insurrection. But these reinforcements were quickly surrounded at Kinsale, and Tyrone suffered a staggering defeat (December 1601) while attempting to break the siege. He continued to resist until forced to surrender on March 30, 1603, six days after the death of Queen Elizabeth.

Elizabeth's successor, King James I, allowed Tyrone to keep most of his lands, but the chieftain soon found that he could not bear the loss of his former independence and prestige. In September 1607 Tyrone, with Rory O'Donnell, Earl of Tyrconnell, and about 100 northern chieftains, secretly embarked on a ship bound for Spain. The vessel was blown off course and landed in the Netherlands. From there the refugees made their way to Rome, where they were acclaimed by Pope Paul V. This "flight of the earls" signaled the end of Gaelic Ulster; thereafter the province was rapidly Anglicized. Outlawed by the English, O'Neill lived in Rome the rest of his life.

became impatient of negotiations with him and finally sent Robert Devereux, 2nd earl of Essex, to Ireland (1599) to subdue him. But Essex lost his reputation by his inglorious progress through the country and by the speed with which he returned to England after a private conversation with O'Neill. Before Charles Blount, Lord Mountjoy, arrived in 1600 to replace Essex, the Irish leaders had gained the qualified support of Pope Clement VIII and of King Philip III of Spain. But Philip could afford to send only a minimal force to aid the Irish rebels. Its leader, Juan del Aguila, occupied Kinsale and was besieged (1601) by Mountjoy. O'Neill marched south to relieve Aguila, but a rash attempt to surprise the English lines by night proved disastrous (December 24, 1601); the Irish were defeated and the Spaniards surrounded. O'Neill held out in Ulster for more than a year but finally submitted a few days after the queen's death in March 1603.

CHAPTER 7

MODERN IRELAND UNDER BRITISH RULE

Viewed generally, Elizabeth's Irish policy had the distinction of having reduced the country to obedience for the first time since the invasion of Henry II. But her policies had serious costs; the loyalty of the Irish was perennially strained over the religious issue, so that further rebellion was almost inevitable (and had been virtually predictable in 1640 when the English government was embarrassed by the Second Bishops' War with Scotland). Economically, the towns and the countryside were needlessly exploited by the new administrators and planters, while the queen's expenditure was substantially increased. Commitments in Ireland were at least partly responsible for the poverty of the crown, which was to become a serious factor in precipitating its 17th-century conflict with Parliament.

THE 17TH CENTURY

James VI of Scotland, who also became King James I of England and Ireland in 1603, pursued a more moderate Irish policy than Elizabeth I, whose commitment to war against the papacy and Catholic Spain impelled her antagonism toward Irish Catholics. But, although James made peace with Spain, his guarded religious toleration was nullified by the intransigence of the established Anglican church and of the papacy.

JAMES I (1603–25)

James, like Elizabeth, bent Irish policy to meet the interests of the English governing class, and the steady exodus of

Irish soldiers and churchmen to Roman Catholic countries in Europe was unabated. In the short term, their absence contributed to peace, but their influence abroad gave the Irish question an international dimension. In Ireland the overwhelming majority of the Gaelic Irish and of the "Old English" (Anglo-Irish) remained detached from government.

As soon as James's policy became clear, the earls of Tyrone and of Tyrconnell and other Ulster Gaelic lords joined the flight from Ireland. Their departure in 1607 opened the way for the plantation of Ulster by a new English and Scottish land-owning class. This proved to be the most successful British settlement in Ireland, because the planters included British tenants and labourers as well as landlords. The newcomers were mainly from the Scottish Lowlands, and the English at first so feared them as competitors that the charter granted to London companies in 1613 added the prefix "London" to the name of the historic ecclesiastical settlement of Derry in an attempt to solidify English holdings. The Presbyterianism of the Scottish immigrants was successfully kept at bay until the time of the English Civil Wars; the Anglican bishoprics in Ireland were well-endowed and powerful, and it was not until 1643 that the first presbytery was established in Belfast.

In the Parliament of 1613–15, which was summoned to ratify the Ulster plantation, a small Protestant majority was achieved because many new boroughs had been created in the newly planted areas. But the government was concerned more with the appearance than the reality of consent, and no Parliament was called again until 1633. In the last years of James's reign, pressure from his Spanish and French allies caused him to concede toleration to the Roman Catholics, and from 1618 a Catholic hierarchy was resident in Ireland.

CHARLES I (1625–49) AND THE COMMONWEALTH (1649–60)

Charles I conceived the idea of raising armies and money in Ireland in return for promises of religious concessions, known as "the Graces," which were designed to secure the status of the Old English by permitting Roman Catholics to engage in various public activities. But this policy was abandoned by Thomas Wentworth, Charles's lord deputy of Ireland from 1633 to 1640 and later the earl of Strafford. Wentworth's authoritarian rule was based on a strategy of manipulating the interests of the planters and the natives, as well as those of the Old English and the New English. He sought to break the power of the great magnates and of trade monopolists, both Irish and English, including the London city companies. He induced the Catholic members of the Irish House of Commons to join in voting large subsidies in the hope of obtaining further concessions. Wentworth's duplicity (most notably his abolition of the remaining Graces), his schemes for further plantations, and his personal enrichment by exploitation of the instruments of state alienated vested interests throughout Ireland. By the time of his impeachment in 1640–41, the loyalty to the crown of even the old landowning classes had been so eroded that the king's enemies in Ireland joined with those in England in bringing about his execution in 1641. His Irish army was disbanded, and control of the Irish government passed to Puritan lords justice.

A general rising of the Irish in Ulster took place in October 1641, and thousands of colonists were murdered or fled. Ulster Catholics and the Old English joined in a confederation—formalized in 1642 as the Confederation of Kilkenny—but it was wracked by dissension. During the English Civil Wars there were Irish confederate armies in Ulster and in Leinster; English parliamentary armies operated in the north and south; and Dublin was held by James Butler, duke of Ormonde, commanding an army of Protestant royalists. Negotiations for peace between Ormonde and the confederates were difficult and protracted, and in 1646, when it was clear that Charles's cause was lost, Ormonde surrendered Dublin to a parliamentary commander. After the execution of Charles in 1649, the English Parliament appointed Oliver Cromwell as commander in chief in Ireland. His nine-month campaign, notorious for the massacre of the garrisons of Drogheda and Wexford, crushed all resistance. By 1652 the conquest of Ireland was complete.

During the Commonwealth and Protectorate (Cromwell's appointment as lord protector was proclaimed in Dublin in 1654), authority in Ireland was exercised by parliamentary commissioners and chief governors. A union of the three kingdoms of England, Scotland, and Ireland, effected in 1653, resulted in Irish representatives' attending Parliaments held in London in 1654, 1656, and 1659. By an Act of Settlement, Ireland, regarded as conquered territory, was parceled out among soldiers and creditors of the Commonwealth, and only those Irish landowners able to prove their constant support of the parliamentary

PROTECTORATE

After the execution of King Charles I, England was declared a commonwealth (1649) under the rule of Parliament. But, after Oliver Cromwell had dissolved the Rump and Barebones parliaments in succession in 1653, he was installed on December 16, 1653, as lord protector of the commonwealth of England, Scotland, and Ireland under the authority of a constitution entitled the Instrument of Government, which had been drawn up by a group of army officers. The Protectorate, as Cromwell's government is now known, was continued after his death on September 3, 1658, by his son Richard, until the latter resigned the office on May 25, 1659, upon which Parliament's resumption of power served merely as a prelude to the Restoration of Charles II.

cause escaped having their estates confiscated. Of these, those who were Roman Catholics were still obliged to exchange land owned to the northeast or south of the River Shannon for land in Connacht (Connaught). Catholics and Anglicans were forbidden to practice their religion, but the campaign against Irish Catholicism was not successful. After the Restoration (1660), Charles II personally favoured complete religious toleration, but the forces of militant Protestantism sometimes proved too strong for him. The Commonwealth parliamentary union was after 1660 treated as null and void.

THE RESTORATION PERIOD AND THE JACOBITE WAR

Most significant of the events of the Restoration was the second Act of Settlement (1662), which enabled Protestants loyal to the crown to recover their estates. The Act of Explanation (1665) obliged the Cromwellian settlers to surrender one-third of their grants and thus provided a reserve of land from which Roman Catholics were partially compensated for losses under the Commonwealth. This satisfied neither group. Catholics were prevented from residing in towns, and local power, in both borough and county, became appropriated to the Protestant interest. But Protestantism itself became permanently split; as in England, the Presbyterians refused to conform to Episcopalian order and practice and, in association with the Presbyterians of Scotland, organized as a separate church.

Under James II, antagonism to the king's Roman Catholicism triggered a reversal of the tendencies of the preceding reign. After his flight from England to France in 1688, James crossed to Ireland, where in Parliament the Acts of Settlement and Explanation were repealed and provision was made for the restoration of expropriated Catholics. When William III landed in Ireland to oppose James, the country divided denominationally, but the real issue was land, not religion. After his defeat at the Battle of the Boyne in 1690, James fled to France, but his Catholic supporters continued in arms until defeated at Aughrim and obliged to surrender in 1691 at Limerick. However, James's supporters secured either the right to go overseas or, if they accepted William's regime, immunity from discriminatory laws. But civil articles to secure toleration for the Catholics were not ratified, and later Irish leaders were thus enabled to denounce the "broken treaty" of Limerick. Immediately after Limerick, the Protestant position was secured by acts of the English Parliament declaring illegal the acts of King James's Parliament in Ireland and restricting to Protestants membership of future Irish Parliaments. The sale of the lands forfeited by James and some of his supporters further reduced the Catholic landownership in the country; by 1703 it was less than 15 percent. On this foundation was established the Protestant Ascendancy.

THE 18TH CENTURY

The Protestant Ascendancy was a supremacy of that proportion of the population, about one-tenth, that belonged to the established Protestant Episcopalian church. They celebrated their position as a ruling class by annual recollections of their victories over their hated popish enemies, especially at the Battle of the Boyne, which has been commemorated on July 12 with parades by the Orange Order from the 1790s until today.

Not only the Catholic majority but also the Presbyterians and other Nonconformists, whose combined numbers exceeded those of the established church, were excluded from full political rights, notably by the Test Act of 1704, which made tenure of office dependent on willingness to receive communion according to the Protestant Episcopalian (Church of Ireland) rite. Because of their banishment from public life, the history of the Roman Catholic Irish in the 18th century is concerned almost exclusively with the activities of exiled soldiers and priests, many of whom distinguished themselves in the service of continental monarchs. Details of the lives of the unrecorded Roman Catholic majority in rural Ireland can be glimpsed only from ephemeral literature in English and from Gaelic poetry.

The Protestant Ascendancy of 18th-century Ireland began in subordination to that of England but ended in asserting its independence. In the 1690s commercial jealousy impelled the Irish Parliament to destroy the Irish woolen export trade, and in 1720 the Declaratory Act affirmed the right of the British Parliament to legislate for Ireland and transferred to the British House of Lords the powers of a supreme court in Irish law cases. By the end of the first quarter of the 18th century, resentment at this subordination had grown sufficiently to enable the celebrated writer Jonathan Swift to whip up a storm of protest in a series of pamphlets over the affair of "Wood's halfpence." William Wood, an English manufacturer, had been authorized to mint coins for Ireland; the outcry against this alleged exploitation by the arbitrary creation of a monopoly became so violent that it could be terminated only by withdrawing the concession from Wood.

Nevertheless, it was another 30 years before a similar protest occurred. In 1751 a group was organized to defeat government resolutions in the Irish Parliament appropriating a financial surplus as the English administrators rather than the Irish legislators saw fit. Although in 1768 the Irish Parliament was made more sensitive to public opinion by a provision for fresh elections every eight years instead of merely at the beginning of a new reign, it remained sufficiently controlled by the government to pass sympathetic resolutions on the revolt of the American colonies.

The American Revolution greatly influenced Irish politics, not least because it removed government troops

JONATHAN SWIFT

Irish author Jonathan Swift (born November 30, 1667, Dublin—died October 19, 1745, Dublin) is arguably the foremost prose satirist in the English language. He was a student at Dublin's Trinity College during the anti-Catholic Revolution of 1688 in England. Irish Catholic reaction in Dublin led Swift, a Protestant, to seek security in England, where he spent various intervals before 1714.

He was ordained an Anglican priest in 1695. His first major work, *A Tale of a Tub* (1704), comprises three satiric sketches on religion and learning; he also became known for religious and political essays and impish pamphlets written under the name "Isaac Bickerstaff." Reluctantly setting aside his loyalty to the Whigs, in 1710 he became the leading writer for the Tories because of their support for the established church. *Journal to Stella* (written 1710–13) consists of letters recording his reactions to the changing world. As a reward for writing and editing Tory publications, in 1713 he was awarded the deanery of St. Patrick's Cathedral, Dublin. He spent nearly all the rest of his life in Ireland, where he devoted himself to exposing English wrongheadedness and their unfair treatment of the Irish. His ironic tract *A Modest Proposal* (1729) proposes ameliorating Irish poverty by butchering children and selling them as food to wealthy English landlords. His famously brilliant and bitter satire *Gulliver's Travels* (1726), ostensibly the story of its hero's encounters with various races and societies in remote regions, reflects Swift's vision of humanity's ambiguous position between bestiality and rationality.

In Jonathan Swift's Gulliver's Travels, *one of Gulliver's first adventures was in the land of Lilliput, as depicted in this illustration from a 19th-century edition of the book.* Apic/ Hulton Archive/Getty Images

from Ireland. Protestant Irish volunteer corps, spontaneously formed to defend the country against possible French attack, exerted pressure for reform. A patriotic opposition led by Henry Flood and Henry Grattan began an agitation that led in 1782 to the repeal of the Declaratory Act of 1720 and to an amendment of Poynings's Law that gave the right of legislative initiative to the Irish Parliament (which under the law was subject to the control of the English king and council). Many of the disadvantages suffered by Roman Catholics in Ireland were abolished, and in 1793 the British government, seeking to win Catholic loyalty on the outbreak of war against revolutionary France, gave them the franchise and admission to most civil offices. The government further attempted to conciliate Catholic opinion in 1795 by founding the seminary of Maynooth to provide education for the Catholic clergy.

But the Protestant Ascendancy resisted efforts to make the Irish Parliament more representative.

The outbreak of the French Revolution had effected a temporary alliance between an intellectual elite among the Presbyterians and leading middle-class Catholics; these groups, under the inspiration of Wolfe Tone, founded in 1791 a radical political club, the Society of United Irishmen, with branches in Belfast and Dublin. After the outbreak of war with revolutionary France, the United Irishmen were suppressed. Reinforced by agrarian malcontents, they regrouped as a secret oath-bound society intent on insurrection.

Wolfe Tone sought military support from France, but a series of French naval expeditions to Ireland between 1796 and 1798 were aborted. The United Irishmen were preparing for rebellion, which broke out in May 1798 but was widespread only

WOLFE TONE

The son of a coach maker, Wolfe Tone (born Theobald Wolfe Tone, June 20, 1763, Dublin—died November 19, 1798, Dublin), studied law and was called to the Irish bar (1789) but soon gave up his practice. In October 1791 he helped found the Society of United Irishmen, initially a predominantly Protestant organization that worked for parliamentary reforms, such as universal suffrage and Roman Catholic emancipation. In Dublin in 1792 he organized a Roman Catholic convention of elected delegates that forced Parliament to pass the Catholic Relief Act of 1793. Tone himself, however, was anticlerical and hoped for a general revolt against religious creeds in Ireland as a sequel to the attainment of Irish political freedom.

By 1794 he and his United Irishmen friends began to seek armed aid from Revolutionary France to help overthrow English rule. After an initial effort failed, Tone went to the United States and obtained letters of introduction from the French minister at Philadelphia to the Committee of Public Safety in Paris. In February 1796 Tone arrived in the French capital, presented his plan for a French invasion of Ireland, and was favourably received. The Directory then appointed one of the most brilliant young French generals, Lazare Hoche, to command the expedition and made Tone an adjutant in the French army.

On December 16, 1796, Tone sailed from Brest with 43 ships and nearly 14,000 men. But the ships were badly handled and, after reaching the coast of west Cork and Kerry, were dispersed by a storm. Tone again brought an Irish invasion plan to Paris in October 1797, but the principal French military leader, Napoleon Bonaparte, took little interest. When insurrection broke out in Ireland in May 1798, Tone could only obtain enough French forces to make small raids on different parts of the Irish coast. In September he entered Lough Swilly, Donegal, with 3,000 men and was captured there.

On November 10 at his trial in Dublin he defiantly proclaimed his undying hostility to England and his desire "in fair and open war to produce the separation of the two countries." Early in the morning of November 12, the day he was to be hanged, he cut his throat with a penknife and died seven days later.

in Ulster and in Wexford in the southeast, where, despite the nonsectarian ideals of its leaders, it assumed a nakedly sectarian form resulting in the slaughter of many Protestants. Although the rebellion failed and was savagely suppressed, the threat to British security posed by the alliance between their French enemies and the Irish rebels prompted the British government to tighten its grip on Ireland. The prime minister, William Pitt the Younger, accordingly planned and carried through an amalgamation of the British and Irish parliaments, merging the two kingdoms into the United Kingdom of Great Britain and Ireland. Despite substantial opposition in the Irish Parliament to its dissolution, the measure passed into law, taking effect on January 1, 1801. To Grattan and his supporters the union of Ireland and Great Britain seemed the end of the Irish nation; the last protest of the United Irishmen was made in Robert Emmet's futile uprising in Dublin in 1803.

SOCIAL, ECONOMIC, AND CULTURAL LIFE IN THE 17TH AND 18TH CENTURIES

Although the late 16th century was marked by the destruction of Gaelic civilization in the upper levels of society, it was preserved among the ordinary people of the northwest, west, and southwest, who continued to speak Irish and who maintained a way of life remote from that of the new landlord class. The 17th-century confiscations made Ireland a land of great estates and, except for Dublin, of small towns decaying under the impact of British restrictions on trade. Except on the Ulster plantations, the tenantry was relatively poor in comparison with that of England and employed inferior agricultural methods. Over large parts of the east and south, tillage farming had given way to pasturage. In the north of Ireland, a similar tendency created a decline in the demand for labour and led in the early 18th century to the migration of substantial numbers of Ulster Scots to North America. In Ulster there gradually emerged a tenantry who compelled their landlords to maintain them in their farms against the claims and bids of Roman Catholic competitors now once again legally entitled to hold land. This purpose immensely strengthened the Orange Order (popularly called the Orangemen), founded in 1795 in defense of the Protestant Ascendancy. Increasingly the Orange Order linked the Protestant gentry and farmers while excluding Catholics from breaking into this privileged ring. Tillage farming was maintained in Ulster more extensively than in the south and west, where there developed on the poorer lands a system of subdivision necessitated by population increase. Apart from folklore and literary sources, little is known of the lives of the ordinary people, and even of the gentry the evidence, apart from estate records, is rarely extensive.

Little need be said of the culture of the Anglo-Irish in the same period, as it followed so closely the traditions of Britain and, very occasionally, those of the rest of Europe. During the 18th century, the new landowning class gradually developed some appreciation of the visual arts. But the really original achievement of the period was in literature, particularly in drama, where the rhetorical gifts of the people secured an audience. In this period there was a strong connection between rhetoric and the arts, as between oratory, themes of social decay, and the consoling power of language and form. Works such as Oliver Goldsmith's *The Deserted Village* and *The Traveller*, Edmund Burke's speeches, and the speeches and plays of Richard Brinsley Sheridan are manifestations of a rhetorical tradition central to Irish feelings.

THE 19TH AND EARLY 20TH CENTURIES

The Act of Union provided that Ireland, as part of the United Kingdom of Great Britain and Ireland, would have 100 members in the House of Commons, about one-fifth of the body's total representation. The union of the churches of England and Ireland as the established denominations of their respective countries was also effected, and the preeminent position in Ireland of Protestant Episcopalianism was further secured by the continuation of the British Test Act, which virtually excluded Nonconformists (both Roman Catholic and Protestant) from Parliament and from membership in municipal corporations. Not until 1828–29 did the repeal of the Test Act and the concession of Catholic emancipation provide political equality for most purposes. It was also provided that there should be free trade between the two countries and that Irish merchandise would be admitted

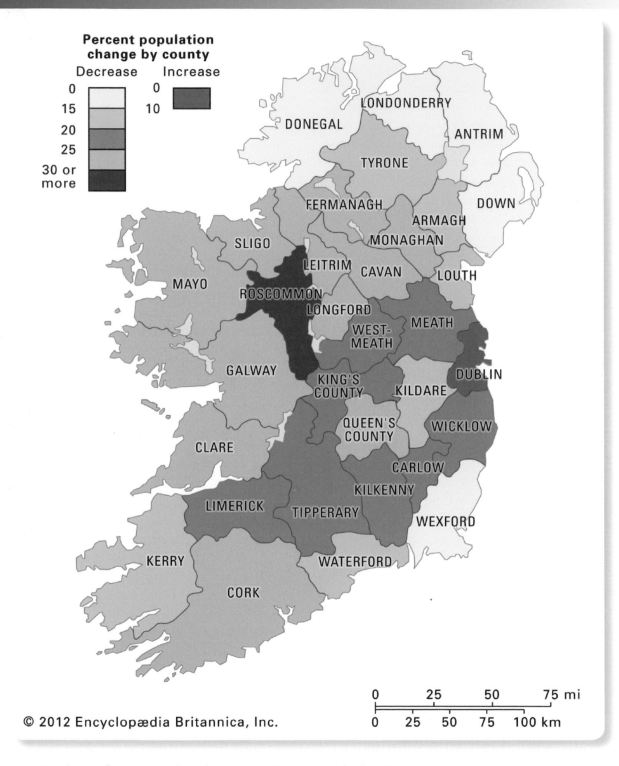

Percent population change by county

Decrease   Increase

0	0
15	10
20	
25	
30 or more	

Population changes in Ireland from 1841 to 1851 as a result of the Great Potato Famine.

to British colonies on the same terms as British merchandise.

But these advantages were not enough to offset the disastrous effect on Ireland of exposure to the full impact of Britain's Industrial Revolution. Within half a century, agricultural produce dropped in value and estate rentals declined, while the rural population increased substantially. When the potato, the staple food of rural Ireland, rotted in the ground as a result of the onset of blight in the mid-1840s, roughly a million people died of starvation and fever in the Irish Potato Famine that ensued, and even more fled abroad. Moreover, emigration continued after the famine ended in 1850. By 1911 Ireland's population was less than half of what it had been before the famine.

POLITICAL DISCONTENT

The Act of Union was motivated not by any concern for the better governance of Ireland but by imperatives of strategic security designed to embed Ireland in a

Victims of the Irish Potato Famine arriving in Liverpool, England; illustration in the Illustrated London News, *July 6, 1850.* © Photos.com/Thinkstock

unitary British state. The Westminster parliament could never be expected to give as much energy and attention to Irish affairs as a parliament in Dublin. Although William Pitt the Younger, mindful of the Roman Catholic Church's animosity toward the French Revolution, had intended to complete the conciliation of Ireland's Catholics by coupling the Act of Union with an act of Catholic emancipation, he was thwarted by the king, George III, who was persuaded that emancipation was incompatible with his coronation oath. The Irish bishops and other potential Catholic supporters of the union were thus disillusioned with the new regime from the outset, and the prospects for political cooperation between Protestant and Catholic conservatives diminished. Bitter sectarian

IRISH POTATO FAMINE

The crop failures of 1845–49 in Ireland that became known as the Irish Potato Famine, or Great Potato Famine, were caused by late blight, a disease that destroys both the leaves and the edible roots, or tubers, of the potato plant. The causative agent of late blight is the water mold *Phytophthora infestans*. The Irish Potato Famine was the worst famine to occur in Europe in the 19th century.

By the early 1840s, almost one-half of the Irish population—but primarily the rural poor—had come to depend almost exclusively on the potato for their diet, and the rest of the population also consumed it in large quantities. A heavy reliance on just one or two high-yielding varieties of potato greatly reduced the genetic variety that ordinarily prevents the decimation of an entire crop by disease, and thus the Irish became vulnerable to famine. In 1845 *Phytophthora* arrived accidentally from North America, and that same year Ireland had unusually cool, moist weather, in which the blight thrived. Much of that year's potato crop rotted in the fields. This partial crop failure was followed by more devastating failures in 1846–49, as each year's potato crop was almost completely ruined by the blight.

The British government's efforts to relieve the famine were inadequate. Prime Minister Sir Robert Peel did what he could to provide relief in 1845 and early 1846, but under the Liberal cabinet of Lord John Russell, which assumed power in June 1846, the emphasis shifted to reliance on Irish resources and the free market, which made disaster inevitable. Much of the financial burden of providing for the starving Irish peasantry was thrown upon the Irish landowners themselves (through local poor relief). But because the peasantry was unable to pay its rents, the landlords soon ran out of funds with which to support them. British assistance was limited to loans, helping to fund soup kitchens, and providing employment on road building and other public works. Cornmeal imported from the United States helped avert some starvation, but it was disliked by the Irish, and reliance on it led to nutritional deficiencies. Despite these shortcomings, by August 1847 as many as three million people were receiving rations at soup kitchens. All in all, the British government spent about £8 million on relief, and some private relief funds were raised as well. Throughout the famine, many Irish farms continued to export grain, meat, and other high-quality foods to Britain because the Irish peasantry lacked the money to purchase them. The government's grudging and ineffective measures to relieve the famine's distress intensified the resentment of British rule among the Irish people.

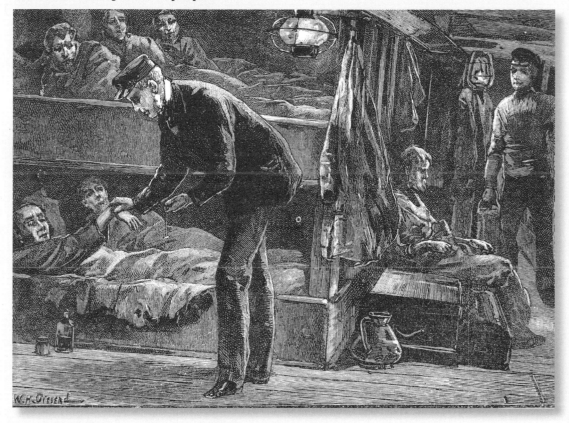

Victims of the Irish Potato Famine immigrating to North America by ship; wood engraving c. 1890. © Photos.com/Thinkstock

The famine proved to be a watershed in the demographic history of Ireland. As a direct consequence of the famine, Ireland's population of almost 8.4 million in 1844 had fallen to 6.6 million by 1851. The number of agricultural labourers and smallholders in the western and southwestern counties underwent an especially drastic decline. About one million people died from starvation or from typhus and other famine-related diseases. The number of Irish who emigrated during the famine may have reached two million. Ireland's population continued to decline in the following decades because of overseas emigration and lower birth rates. By the time Ireland achieved independence in 1921, its population was barely half of what it had been in the early 1840s.

antagonisms—resurrected by the slaughter of both Protestants and Catholics in the 1798 rebellion and its no-less-bloody aftermath—reinforced the likelihood that the political divide would mirror the religious. That likelihood became a certainty in 1823 when the formation of the Catholic Association transmuted the demand for emancipation into a mass political movement that commanded attention throughout Europe. The emergence of the Catholic barrister Daniel O'Connell as the founding father and popular champion of Catholic democracy, along with the dramatic manner in which he was elected to a parliamentary seat for County Clare (1828), forced the grudging concession of the Catholic Emancipation Act of 1829 by a government fearful of popular upheaval. The reaction among alarmed Protestants and their apprehension that emancipation might open the door for the Catholic majority ultimately to achieve ascendancy led to an alliance between the Presbyterians and their old oppressors, the Protestant Episcopalians. Middle-class Catholics and Protestants drifted apart, the latter increasingly clinging to the union and the former more slowly but at last decisively coming to seek its repeal.

O'Connell's next great campaign was for the repeal of the union, but, although he had been able to muster support for emancipation from the more liberal elements of British political opinion, no such support was forthcoming for repeal. O'Connell resorted to organizing "monster meetings," huge open-air demonstrations at sites of historical significance throughout Ireland. A climax was reached in October 1843 when troops and artillery were called out to suppress the mass meeting arranged at Clontarf, outside Dublin. O'Connell canceled the meeting to avoid the risk of bloodshed; his method of popular agitation within the law thus proved unavailing, and his influence thereafter rapidly declined.

Associated with O'Connell's repeal agitation was the Young Ireland movement, a group connected with a repeal weekly newspaper, *The Nation*, and led by its editor, Charles Gavan Duffy, its chief contributor Thomas Osborne Davis, and its special land correspondent, John Blake Dillon. They became increasingly restless at O'Connell's cautious policy after Clontarf, however, and in 1848 became involved in an inept rising. Its failure, and the deportation or escape from Ireland of most of the Young Ireland leaders, destroyed the repeal movement.

For about 20 years after the Irish Potato Famine, political agitation was subdued, and emigration continued to reduce the population every year. The landowners also suffered severely from an inability to collect rents, and there was a wholesale transfer of estates to new owners. Evictions were widespread, and cottages were demolished at once by the landlords to prevent other impoverished tenants from occupying them. The flow of emigrants to the United States was encouraged by invitations from Irish

DANIEL O'CONNELL

Compelled to leave the Roman Catholic college at Douai, France, when the French Revolution broke out, Daniel O'Connell (born August 6, 1775, near Cahirciveen, County Kerry, Ireland—died May 15, 1847, Genoa, Kingdom of Sardinia [Italy]) went to London to study law, and in 1798 he was called to the Irish bar. His forensic skill enabled him to use the courts as nationalist forums. Although he had joined the Society of United Irishmen, a revolutionary society, as early as 1797, he refused to participate in the Irish Rebellion of the following year. When the Act of Union (which took effect January 1, 1801) abolished the Irish Parliament, he insisted that the British Parliament repeal the anti-Catholic laws in order to justify its claim to represent the people of Ireland. From 1813 he opposed various Catholic relief proposals because the government, with the acquiescence of

Daniel O'Connell. © Photos.com/Thinkstock

the papacy, would have had the right to veto nominations to Catholic bishoprics in Great Britain and Ireland. Although permanent political organizations of Catholics were illegal, O'Connell set up a nationwide series of mass meetings to petition for Catholic emancipation.

On May 12, 1823, O'Connell and Richard Lalor Sheil (1791–1851) founded the Catholic Association, which quickly attracted the support of the Irish priesthood and of lawyers and other educated Catholic laymen and which eventually comprised so many members that the government could not suppress it. In 1826, when it was reorganized as the New Catholic Association, it caused the defeat of several parliamentary candidates sponsored by large landowners. In County Clare in July 1828, O'Connell himself, although (as a Catholic) ineligible to sit in the House of Commons, defeated a man who tried to support both the British government and Catholic emancipation. This result impressed on the British prime minister, Arthur Wellesley, 1st duke of Wellington, the need for making a major concession to the Irish Catholics. Following the passage of the Catholic Emancipation Act of 1829, O'Connell, after going through the formality of an uncontested reelection, took his seat at Westminster.

In April 1835 he helped to overthrow Sir Robert Peel's Conservative ministry, and in the same year he entered into the "Lichfield House compact," whereby he promised the Whig Party leaders a period of "perfect calm" in Ireland while the government enacted reform measures. O'Connell and his Irish adherents (known collectively as "O'Connell's tail") then aided in keeping the weak Whig administration of William Lamb, 2nd Viscount Melbourne, in office from 1835 to 1841. By 1839, however, O'Connell realized that the Whigs would do little more than the Conservatives for Ireland, and in 1840 he founded the Repeal Association to dissolve the Anglo-Irish legislative union. A series of mass meetings in all parts of Ireland culminated in O'Connell's arrest for seditious conspiracy, but he was released on appeal after three months' imprisonment (June–September 1844). Afterward his health failed rapidly, and the nationalist leadership fell to the radical Young Ireland group.

people already there, and in England the new industrial cities and shipping centres attracted large settlements of poor migrants from Ireland.

THE RISE OF FENIANISM

Among the exiles both in the United States and in Britain, the Fenian movement spread widely. A secret revolutionary society named for the Fianna, an Irish armed force of legendary times, it aimed at securing Ireland's independence by exploiting every opportunity to injure British interests and, ultimately, to break the British connection.

In Ireland, Fenian ideals were propagated in the newspaper *The Irish People*, and in 1865 four Fenian leaders—Charles Joseph Kickham, John O'Leary, Thomas Clarke Luby, and Jeremiah O'Donovan Rossa—were sentenced to long-term imprisonment for publishing treasonable documents. During the next two years, plans gradually developed for a projected nationwide rising, financed largely by funds collected in the United States. It took place in March 1867 but was easily crushed and its leaders imprisoned. The prime minister, William Ewart Gladstone, at last recognizing the necessity for drastic Irish reforms, disestablished the Protestant Church of Ireland in 1869 and in 1870 introduced the first Irish Land Act, which conceded the principles of secure tenure and compensation for improvements made to property.

THE HOME RULE MOVEMENT AND THE LAND LEAGUE

In 1870 a constitutional movement seeking domestic self-government, the Home

Government Association (Home Rule League), was founded by Isaac Butt, a prominent unionist lawyer interested in land reform. In the election of 1874, it returned about 60 members to Parliament. The movement was tolerated rather than encouraged by the various groups of Irish nationalists, and it was not fully supported by the Roman Catholic clergy until the 1880s.

A return of bad harvests in 1879 brought new fears of famine. That same year, Michael Davitt founded the Irish Land League, seeking to achieve for tenants security of tenure, fair rents, and freedom to sell property. A formidable agrarian agitation developed when Davitt joined forces with Charles Stewart Parnell, a young Protestant landowner and member of Parliament in the Home Rule Party, which soon elected him as its leader in place of Butt. Parnell undertook a tour of North America to raise funds for the Land League. There he was influenced by two Irish Americans: John Devoy, a leading member of Clan na Gael, an effective American Fenian organization, and Patrick Ford, whose New York paper *The Irish World* preached militant republicanism and hatred of England. At Westminster Parnell adopted a policy of persistent obstruction, which compelled attention to Irish needs by bringing parliamentary business to a standstill. Gladstone was forced to introduce his Land Act of 1881, conceding fixity of tenure, fair rents, and free sale of the tenant's interest.

Parnell's success was not achieved without serious difficulties, including the ultimate proscription of the Land League by the government and the imprisonment of its leaders. As a result, Parnell used his parliamentary party, then increased to 86 seats, to overthrow Gladstone's Liberal government. But the disclosure of Gladstone's conversion to Home Rule—after the 1885 general election had given Parnell's party control of the balance of power in the House of Commons—signaled the greatest change in the political landscape since 1800. The bipartisan consensus between British political parties on the indissolubility of the constitutional relationship between the two islands, explicitly declared irrevocable under the terms of the Act of Union, collapsed. When Lord Salisbury's short-lived Conservative government rejected Gladstone's proposal for a new bipartisan settlement of the Irish question in January 1886, the Act of Union became the most divisive issue in British politics. Although Gladstone's first Home Rule Bill of 1886 split his party and was defeated by an alliance of Conservative and Liberal unionists in the House of Commons, that divide remained until the outbreak of World War I in 1914.

There followed 20 years when the aspirations of Irish constitutional nationalists were frustrated, partly because the Conservatives (now called the Conservative and Unionist Party) were mainly in power and partly because the Home Rule Party split after Parnell's involvement (1889) in a divorce suit. The split was prompted by pressure from Gladstone and from the Irish Catholic

LAND LEAGUE

The Land League was founded in October 1879 by Michael Davitt, the son of an evicted tenant farmer and a member of the Fenian (Irish Republican) Brotherhood. Davitt asked Charles Stewart Parnell, leader of the Irish Home Rule Party in the British Parliament, to preside over the league; this linking of the land reform movement with parliamentary activity constituted a new departure in the Irish national movement.

The league's program was based upon the "three F's": fair rent, fixity of tenure, and free sale of the right of occupancy. The passage in 1881 of Gladstone's Land Act, restricting the privileges of landlords, was a victory for the league. Parnell's increasingly violent speeches, however, led to his arrest on October 13, 1881, and the league called on tenants to withhold all rents. The government used this "no-rent manifesto" as a pretext for its suppression of the league on October 20.

bishops for Parnell to relinquish his party leadership. Meanwhile, Gladstone's second Home Rule Bill (1893) was rejected in the House of Lords, where the Conservatives enjoyed a permanent majority. Only in 1900 was a Parnellite, John Redmond, able to reunite the party. In the last years of the century, partly in reaction to political frustrations, a cultural nationalist movement developed, led by Douglas Hyde and Eoin MacNeill. Through the Gaelic League (founded in 1893) much was done to revive interest in the speaking and study of Irish. These cultural movements were reinforced by a radical nationalist party, Sinn Féin ("We Ourselves"), founded in 1905 by Arthur Griffith, who preached a doctrine of political self-help. It subsequently emerged that a Fenian organization, the Irish Republican Brotherhood, had revived and was secretly recruiting membership through various cultural societies and through the Gaelic Athletic Association, founded in 1884 to promote specifically Irish sports.

At the close of the century, the Conservatives initiated a policy designed to "kill Home Rule by kindness" by introducing constructive reforms in Ireland. Their most important achievement was the Land Purchase Act of 1903, which initiated the greatest social revolution in Ireland since the 17th century. By providing generous inducements to landlords to sell their estates, the act effected by government mediation the transfer of landownership to the occupying tenants.

THE 20TH-CENTURY CRISIS

Disillusioned by the defeats of the 1886 and 1893 Home Rule bills, the Liberals ignored the demand for Home Rule when they won an overall majority in the 1906 election. But Ireland came to the top of the political agenda when two elections in 1910, caused by a constitutional crisis regarding the powers of the House of Lords, made the Liberal government of H.H. Asquith dependent on the Home Rule Party for its parliamentary majority. The reduction of the power of the Lords by the Parliament Act of 1911 seemed to promise that the third Home Rule bill, introduced in 1912, would come into force by the summer of 1914. But, in the meantime, the Irish unionists, under their charismatic leader, Edward Carson, had mounted an effective extraparliamentary campaign backed by Bonar Law, the leader of the Conservative Party. Thousands of Ulstermen signed the Solemn League and Covenant to resist Home Rule (1912), and in January 1913 the Ulster unionists established a paramilitary army, the Ulster Volunteer Force (UVF), to coordinate armed resistance. In September 1913 Carson announced that a provisional government of Ulster would be established in the event of Home Rule's coming into effect. After at first seeking to reject Home Rule for all of Ireland, the unionists gradually fell back on a demand for Ulster (where unionists were predominant) to be excluded from its scope. Redmond's claim that there was "no Ulster question" and Asquith's public, albeit disingenuous, refusal to contemplate Ulster's exclusion from the terms of the bill hardened the Protestant and unionist resistance in the areas around Belfast. Of the nine Ulster counties, Down, Antrim, Armagh, and Derry (Londonderry) had unionist majorities; Donegal, Cavan, and Monaghan had strong Home Rule majorities; and Tyrone and Fermanagh had small Home Rule majorities. The boasts of the 90,000-strong UVF that it enjoyed active sympathy in the British army became plausible when the officers in the cavalry brigade at The Curragh suddenly announced in March 1914 that they would resign if ordered to move against the UVF. Meanwhile, a nationalist force, the Irish Volunteers, had been launched in Dublin in November 1913 to counter the UVF. Both forces gathered arms, and Ireland seemed close to civil war when World War I broke out. Assured of Redmond's support in recruiting for the army, Asquith enacted the third Home Rule Bill but accompanied it with a Suspensory Act, postponing its implementation until the return of peace.

World War I restored bipartisanship on Irish policy, as all differences between the Liberals and Conservatives were subordinated to the goal of defeating Germany. Coalition governments—first under Asquith in 1915–16 and from 1916–22 under David Lloyd George—destroyed the leverage exerted by the Home Rule party's control of the balance of power in the Commons since 1910. Initial enthusiasm for the war and Redmond's popularity in the wake of Home Rule's enactment prompted a large majority—some 150,000 "National Volunteers," as opposed to fewer than 10,000 antiwar "Irish Volunteers" (who were secretly manipulated by the revolutionary Irish Republican Brotherhood)—to endorse Redmond's support for the war. But the longer the war dragged on, the more the revolutionary element gained support

EASTER RISING

The Easter Rising (or Easter Rebellion), which began on Easter Monday, April 24, 1916, in Dublin, was planned by Patrick Pearse, Tom Clarke, and several other leaders of the Irish Republican Brotherhood. The Brotherhood was a revolutionary society within the nationalist organization called the Irish Volunteers, the latter of which had about 16,000 members and was armed with German weapons smuggled into the country in 1914. These two organizations were supplemented by the Irish Citizen Army, an association of Dublin workers formed after the failure of the general strike of 1913, and by the small Sinn Féin party.

The uprising was planned to be nationwide in scope, but a series of mishaps led to its being confined to Dublin alone. The British had learned of the planned uprising and on April 21 arrested Irish nationalist Sir Roger Casement in County Kerry for running arms for the rebels. Eoin MacNeill, the leader of the Irish Volunteers, therefore canceled mobilization orders for the insurgents, but Pearse and Clarke went ahead with about 1,560 Irish Volunteers and a 200-man contingent of the Citizen Army. On April 24 their forces seized the Dublin General Post Office and other strategic points in Dublin's city centre, and Pearse read aloud a proclamation announcing the birth of the Irish republic. British troops soon arrived to put down the rebellion, and for nearly a week Dublin was paralyzed by street fighting. British artillery bombardments compelled Pearse and his colleagues to surrender on April 29.

Pearse and 14 other leaders of the rebellion were court-martialed and executed by British authorities in the weeks that followed. Though the uprising itself had been unpopular with most of the Irish people, these executions excited a wave of revulsion against the British authorities and turned the dead republican leaders into martyred heroes. The Easter Rising signaled the start of the republican revolution in Ireland. Because Eamon de Valera was the senior survivor of the rising, he gained much of his personal popularity with the Irish people from that event.

from those alienated by Redmond's pro-British attitude. Before the end of 1914 the Irish Republican Brotherhood made full plans for a revolutionary outbreak. When the rising took place, on Easter Monday 1916, only about 1,000 men and women were actually engaged. A provisional Irish government was proclaimed. The General Post Office and other parts of Dublin were seized; street fighting continued for about a week until Tom Clarke, Patrick Pearse, and other republican leaders were forced to surrender.

The execution of Clarke and Pearse inflamed nationalist opinion and, compounded by the threat that conscription would be introduced in Ireland, led to the defeat and virtual extinction of Redmond's Irish Parlimentary Party in the general election of December 1918. Their successful opponents, calling themselves Sinn Féin and supporting the republican program announced in 1916, were led by Eamon de Valera, a surviving leader of the Easter Rising, who campaigned for Irish independence in the United States as "president of the Irish Republic." The republicans refused to take their seats in the Westminster Parliament but instead set up their provisional government, elected by the Irish members of Parliament at a meeting in Dublin called Dáil Éireann ("Irish Assembly)," which sought to provide an alternative to British administration and which first met on January 21, 1919. Simultaneously, the Irish Republican Army (IRA) was organized to resist British administration and to secure recognition for the government of the Irish republic. There followed a guerrilla war: the Anglo-Irish War, also known as the Irish War of Independence.

The IRA launched widespread ambushes and attacks on police barracks, while British forces retaliated with ruthless reprisals. A large proportion of the Irish police resigned and were replaced by British recruits, who became known as Black and Tans for their temporary uniforms of dark tunics and khaki trousers.

The 1918 election had made Lloyd George's government dependent on the Conservatives for its majority in the Commons and, when the Home Rule legislation of 1914 was disinterred, this ensured separate treatment for Ulster. The Government of Ireland Act (1920) split Ireland into two self-governing areas, both with devolved powers approximating to Home Rule. Northern Ireland consisted of six counties (Antrim, Down, Armagh, Derry, Fermanagh, and Tyrone), the largest number in which the Ulster Unionists were assured of a

BLACK AND TANS

When Irish republican agitation intensified after World War I, many Irish policeman stepped down. From January 1920 to July 1921, their places were taken by temporary British recruits (mostly jobless former soldiers) who enrolled in the Royal Irish Constabulary (RIC). Not only were these recruits paid a mere 10 shillings a day, but because of a shortage of standard uniforms, they were issued makeshift uniforms made up of green police tunics and khaki military trousers. This ensemble resembled the distinctive markings of a famous pack of Limerick foxhounds and earned the force the name the Black and Tans.

In seeking to counter the terrorism of the Irish Republican Army (IRA), the Black and Tans themselves engaged in brutal reprisals. Notably, on "Bloody Sunday," November 21, 1920, the IRA killed 11 Englishmen suspected of being intelligence agents. The Black and Tans took revenge the same afternoon, attacking spectators at a Gaelic football match in Croke Park, Dublin, killing 12 and wounding 60. The RIC was disbanded in 1922 after the Anglo-Irish Treaty of December 1921.

permanent majority. Southern Ireland consisted of the remaining 26 counties, including the three Ulster counties with clear nationalist-Catholic majorities (Donegal, Cavan, and Monaghan). Sinn Féin rejected the act as incompatible with its republican aspirations, and it never came into force in "Southern Ireland." But Sinn Féin could do nothing to resist partition, which became a reality with the first meetings of the government and parliament of Northern Ireland in Belfast in June 1921.

A truce in July 1921 ended the Anglo-Irish War and initiated exchanges between Lloyd George and de Valera, which were protracted because neither side would admit the other's legality. But negotiations in London, which began in October, culminated in the Anglo-Irish Treaty, signed on December 6, 1921, on behalf of the United Kingdom by Lloyd George and leading members of his cabinet and on behalf of Ireland by Arthur Griffith, Michael Collins, and other members of the republican cabinet.

CHAPTER 8

INDEPENDENT IRELAND

The end of the Irish War of Independence (Anglo-Irish War) brought a large measure of sovereignty for most of the island but did not bring lasting peace. In short order a civil war would be fought to determine the future of the Irish state, and the six counties of the north, which remained within the United Kingdom as Northern Ireland, would be beset with political turmoil and violence into the 21st century. Yet Ireland would find its place among the world's community of nations and, eventually, as one of the members of the European Union.

1922 TO 1959

The nearly four decades that stretched between the Anglo-Irish Treaty and Eamon de Valera's assumption of the presidency of the Republic of Ireland were a trying but exciting era for the Irish. It was a time of great changes and great leaders, none of whom were more dynamic than de Valera, arguably Ireland's preeminent statesman.

THE IRISH FREE STATE, 1922–32

The Irish Free State, established under the terms of the treaty with the same constitutional status as Canada and the other dominions in the British Commonwealth, came into existence on December 6, 1922. The Anglo-Irish Treaty (Article 12) also stated that Northern Ireland could opt out of the Irish Free State and provided for a commission to establish a permanent frontier. Despite Northern Ireland's reluctance, the Boundary Commission was set up and sat in secret session during 1924–25. But when it recommended only minor changes, which all three governments rejected as less satisfactory than maintaining the status quo, the tripartite intergovernmental agreement of December 3, 1925, revoked the commission's powers and maintained the existing boundary of Northern Ireland.

The treaty triggered bitter dissension in Sinn Féin, and some of its terms—notably the prescribed oath of allegiance to the British crown—were so repugnant to many republicans, led by de Valera, that the Dáil ratified the treaty on January 7, 1922, by only seven votes: 64 to 57. De Valera's resignation as president signaled his refusal to accept that vote as a final verdict and enhanced the respectability of opposition to the treaty despite its endorsement in an election on June 16, 1922. The IRA also split, with a majority of its members (known as the Irregulars) opposed to the treaty. There followed a bitter civil war that cost almost 1,000 lives. The most famous casualty was Michael Collins, the charismatic guerrilla leader and chairman of the 1922 Provisional Government (set up to implement the treaty), who was killed in an ambush in Cork on August 22, 1922. He was succeeded by the more prosaic William T. Cosgrave, who became the first head of government ("president of the Executive Council") of the Irish Free

William Thomas Cosgrave. George Grantham Bain Collection/Library of Congress, Washington, D.C. (Digital File Number: LC-DIG-ggbain-35309)

State. The victory of Cosgrave's government in the civil war was never in doubt: its electoral majority, the Catholic hierarchy's condemnation of the Irregulars, and such draconian measures as internment without trial and the introduction of the death penalty for possession of arms (77 republicans were executed), as well as factionalism within their own ranks, doomed the Irregulars to defeat, although they did not suspend military operations until April 27, 1923.

In the election of August 1923, Cosgrave's party, Cumann na nGaedheal ("Party of the Irish"), won 63 seats, as opposed to 44 for de Valera's Sinn Féin party; however, Sinn Féin abdicated its role as main opposition party when its elected members refused to sit in the new Dáil. Sinn Féin's absence enhanced the authority of Cosgrave's government and enabled the speedy enactment of the mass of legislation necessary to set the infant state on firm foundations.

The cost of postwar reconstruction was immense. In 1923–24, 30 percent of all national expenditure went toward defense and another 7 percent was allocated to compensation for property losses and personal injuries. Yet despite such economic difficulties, the government pursued an efficient farming policy and carried through important hydroelectric projects. Administration was increasingly centralized; an efficient civil service based on the British model and copper-fastened against corruption was established; and Kevin O'Higgins, as minister for justice, carried through many judicial reforms.

In the general election of June 1927, Cosgrave's support in the Dáil was further reduced, but he nevertheless formed a new ministry, in which O'Higgins became vice president of the Executive Council. O'Higgins's assassination by maverick republicans on July 10 suddenly revived old feuds. Cosgrave

passed a stringent Public Safety Act and introduced legislation requiring that all candidates for the Dáil declare their willingness, if elected, to take the oath of allegiance. De Valera then led his new party, Fianna Fáil ("Soldiers of Ireland"), into the Dáil and signed the declaration required under the oath of allegiance, which he now claimed was "merely an empty political formula" that did not involve its signatories in "obligations of loyalty to the English Crown."

De Valera's commitment to constitutional politics and Fianna Fáil's assumption of the role of parliamentary opposition posed insuperable electoral problems for Cumann na nGaedheal. The civil war split permanently shaped party politics in independent Ireland. It ensured that the British connection, as embodied in the treaty, replaced the Act of Union as the great divide: pro-treaty against antitreaty replaced unionist versus nationalist as the hallmarks of political commitment. Although Collins had described the treaty merely as a "stepping stone," a means to the end of greater independence, the blood spilled in the civil war locked his successors in Cumann na nGaedheal (which joined with two lesser parties—the Centre Party and the Blue Shirts—to form Fine Gael in 1933) into seeing the treaty as an end in itself and denied them the access enjoyed by Fianna Fáil to the reservoir of anti-British sentiment that remained the most potent force in Irish nationalist politics. The problems of Cosgrave's last administration were compounded

BLUESHIRTS

Known popularly as the Blueshirts for the coloured shirts they had adopted in imitation of the European fascist movements, the Army Comrades Association (ACA) was founded in response to the victory of Fianna Fáil in the 1932 election and was led by Gen. Eoin O'Duffy, former commissioner of the Irish Civic Guard (An Garda Síochána). Initially composed of former soldiers in the Irish Free State Army, the ACA was renamed the National Guard in 1933 and later that year merged with Cumann na nGaedheal ("Party of the Irish") and the Centre Party to form Fine Gael, thereafter the principal opposition party. O'Duffy served briefly as its leader. In 1936 O'Duffy took some 600 Blueshirts to Spain, where they fought as the "Irish brigade" with the Nationalist forces during the Spanish Civil War.

Irish fascist leader Eoin O'Duffy stands at the centre at a rally of his Blueshirts, circa *1935.* Hulton Archive/Getty Images

by the Great Depression (triggered by the U.S. stock market crash of 1929), and the resulting unemployment and general discontent with the government led to its defeat in February 1932. Fianna Fáil won enough seats for de Valera, with Labour Party support, to be able to form a new government.

DE VALERA'S GOVERNMENTS (1932–48) AND THE QUEST FOR SOVEREIGNTY

De Valera's primary purpose was to expunge those elements of the treaty he thought restrictive of Irish independence. His obsession with British-Irish relations was reflected in his holding the ministerial portfolio for external affairs simultaneously with the presidency of the Executive Council. He moved first to abolish the oath of allegiance, although the Senate's opposition delayed the enactment of the necessary legislation until May 1933. His government also degraded the office of Britain's governor-general in Ireland by systematically humiliating its incumbent, James McNeill; exploiting the constitutional doctrine that the British sovereign must act on ministerial advice, de Valera counseled the dismissal of McNeil (which occurred in November 1932) and forced his replacement by a subservient supporter. He also stopped the transfer to the British treasury of the land annuities, repayments of the loans advanced to Irish

Eamon de Valera. Encyclopædia Britannica, Inc.

tenant farmers to buy their land under the Land Acts of 1891–1909. In July 1932 the British imposed import duties on most Irish exports to the United Kingdom to recoup their losses, and the Irish retaliated in kind. Although the British were financial beneficiaries in the "economic war," Fianna Fáil was the political beneficiary because it cloaked its protectionist policies in patriotic rhetoric and blamed Britain for the deepening recession; it duly won an overall majority in the snap election called by de Valera in January 1933.

In December 1936 de Valera seized on the abdication of Edward VIII to enact two bills: the first deleted all mention of the king and the governor-general from the 1922 constitution; the second, the External Relations Act, gave effect to the abdication and recognized the crown only for the purposes of diplomatic representation. De Valera's new constitution, ratified by referendum, came into effect on December 29, 1937, and made "Ireland"—the new name of the state ("Éire" in Irish, which was now proclaimed the first official language)—an independent republic associated with the British Commonwealth only as matter of external policy. The head of state was henceforth a president elected by popular vote to a seven-year term, and the head of government was the taoiseach (prime minister). De Valera's achievement was extraordinary: acting unilaterally, he had rewritten the constitutional relationship with Britain in less than six years. But he had to negotiate with British Prime Minster Neville Chamberlain's government to achieve his remaining objective: the transfer of three naval bases occupied by the British under a defense annex to the treaty. This he achieved with the defense agreement of April 25, 1938, which was coupled with a finance agreement (settling the land annuities dispute) and a trade agreement (softening the tariff war). The defense agreement completed the process of establishing Irish sovereignty and made possible Ireland's neutrality in a European war, an avowed republican aspiration since the 1921 treaty negotiations.

At the outbreak of World War II, de Valera renewed his statement, made in 1938, that Ireland would not become a base for attacks on Great Britain. Under the Emergency Powers Act of 1939, hundreds of IRA members were interned without trial, and six were executed between 1940 and 1944. Ostensibly, de Valera's government, reelected in 1943 and 1944, remained strictly neutral, despite pressure from British Prime Minister Winston Churchill, German air raids on Dublin in 1941, and, after the United States entered the war in December 1941, pressure from U.S. Pres. Franklin D. Roosevelt. But, secretly, the Irish authorities provided significant intelligence and other assistance to the Allies because de Valera realized that a German victory would threaten that hard-won independence of which Irish neutrality was the ultimate expression.

THE REPUBLIC OF IRELAND

In the general election of 1948, Fianna Fáil failed to gain a majority, winning only 68 of the 147 seats in the Dáil, but de Valera refused to enter a coalition. John A. Costello emerged as the leader of an interparty government led by his own

SEÁN F. LEMASS

Seán F. Lemass (born July 15, 1899, Dublin—died May 11, 1971, Dublin) served as taoiseach from 1959 to 1966. As early as the age of 16, Lemass became a freedom fighter in the streets of Dublin, engaging in the Easter Rising (April 1916) and other hostilities and landing in jail again and again. He opposed the establishment of the Irish Free State as a dominion under the Anglo-Irish Treaty of 1921 and became a member of the headquarters staff of the Irish Republican Army in the civil war of 1922–23. He played a key role in persuading Eamon de Valera to found a new republican party, Fianna Fáil, in 1926. After de Valera rose to the premiership in 1932, Lemass held portfolios in all his cabinets for 21 of the next 27 years, notably as minister of industry and commerce and then as *tánaiste* (deputy prime minister).

When de Valera became president in 1959, Lemass inherited the office of taoiseach. Under him the country took a more outward-looking approach, and he especially pressed for Ireland's entry into the European Economic Community (EEC, now the European Community, embedded in the European Union) and for reconciliation with Northern Ireland. Ill health, however, forced him to relinquish the leadership of his party in 1966, and he withdrew from politics in 1969. His greatest legacy, Ireland's membership in the EEC, was not secured until 1973, after his death.

party, Fine Gael. Costello introduced the Republic of Ireland Act, which repealed the External Relations Act of 1936 and ended the fiction of Commonwealth membership. The act took effect in April 1949, and the British government retaliated with legislation recognizing the new status of Ireland but guaranteeing the constitutional status of Northern Ireland and the territorial integrity of Northern Ireland as subject to the consent of the parliament of Northern Ireland. Although partition remained a festering sore that erupted 20 years later, the Republic of Ireland Act dissolved the obsession with the British connection. Henceforth relations between Dublin and London were conducted on the basis of absolute equality between sovereign governments, and

domestic politics, as elsewhere in western Europe, increasingly became the politics of economics.

The 1950s were a time of economic stagnation (with emigration running at levels unprecedented since the 1880s) and of political flux. There were changes of government after the elections of 1951, 1954, and 1957, when Fianna Fáil returned to power for what proved to be another 16 years. In 1959 a blind and aging de Valera was elected president, and he remained in that office until 1973. His successor as taoiseach (1959–66) was Seán Lemass— minister for industry and commerce (1932–39, 1941–48, 1951–54, 1957–59), as well as minister for supplies during World War II—whose predominant interest had always been economics.

SINCE 1959

Economic Development, a plan for national regeneration, had been published in 1958 under the name of T.K. Whitaker, an exceptional civil servant and then secretary of the Department of Finance. Lemass and Whitaker implemented the First Programme for Economic Expansion (1958–63), under which the principle of protection was abandoned and foreign investment encouraged, while a targeted growth rate of 2 percent resulted in 4 percent actual growth. This prosperity brought profound social and cultural changes to what had been one of the poorest countries in Europe. Emigration substantially declined; access to education broadened; consumer spending increased, and holidaying abroad became commonplace; Catholic social teaching was challenged; and the advent of an Irish television service eroded traditional values and led to a relaxation of censorship of books and films.

INTEGRATION IN EUROPE

In 1961 Ireland applied for membership of the European Economic Community (EEC; later the European Community [EC], embedded in the European Union [EU]). The application lapsed when the French vetoed Britain's entry; the predominance of the British market for Irish producers was such that it made no sense for Ireland to join the EEC if Britain was excluded. Nevertheless, Lemass's unequivocal commitment to Europe (for which he won the support of the main opposition party, Fine Gael) proved his enduring legacy. The Anglo-Irish Free Trade Area Agreement of 1965 dismantled more tariff barriers, and although Ireland, like Britain, did not join the EEC until January 1, 1973, the delay eased the impact of transition.

Engagement in Europe transformed Ireland socially as well as economically. Production subsidies and higher prices under the EEC's Common Agricultural Policy (CAP) benefitted Irish farmers; Irish industry gained from access to wider markets; and European social and regional programs revolutionized the country's infrastructure. Reduced dependence on British markets led in 1979 to Ireland's joining the European Monetary System despite Britain's staying outside it; this severance of the more than 150-year link with sterling was affirmed in 2002 when Ireland, unlike Britain, joined the euro zone (the countries that share the euro as their currency). In May 1987 a constitutional referendum ratified the Single European Act and confirmed Ireland's participation in the EEC. The act called for the harmonization of social and fiscal measures taken within the EEC and was a forerunner of the 1991 Maastricht Treaty (Treaty on European Union), which paved the way for the establishment of economic and monetary union and was approved by a large majority of Irish voters in a referendum. Ireland became an unexpected obstacle to further European integration, however, when the Lisbon Treaty—an agreement aimed at

EUROPEAN COMMUNITY

The European Economic Community (EEC) was created in 1957 by the Treaty of Rome, which was signed by Belgium, France, Italy, Luxembourg, the Netherlands, and West Germany. The United Kingdom, Denmark, and Ireland joined in 1973, followed by Greece in 1981 and Portugal and Spain in 1986. The former East Germany was admitted as part of reunified Germany in 1990.

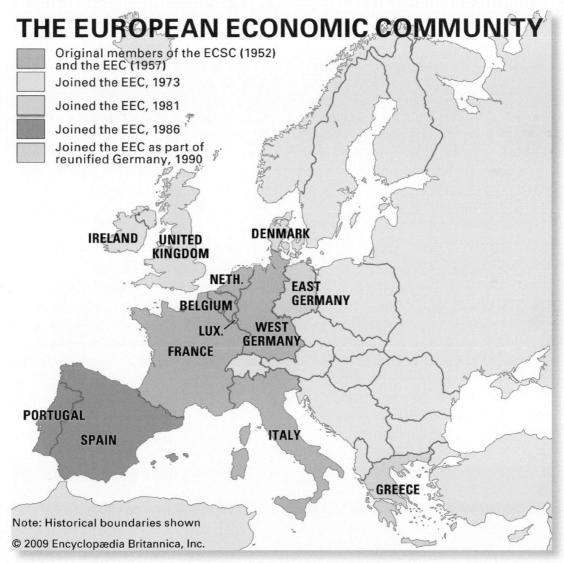

THE EUROPEAN ECONOMIC COMMUNITY

Original members of the ECSC (1952) and the EEC (1957)

Joined the EEC, 1973

Joined the EEC, 1981

Joined the EEC, 1986

Joined the EEC as part of reunified Germany, 1990

Note: Historical boundaries shown

© 2009 Encyclopædia Britannica, Inc.

Map showing the composition of the European Economic Community (EEC) from 1957, when it was formed by the members of the European Coal and Steel Community (ECSC), to 1993, when it was renamed the European Community (EC) and was subsumed under the European Union (EU).

The EEC was designed to create a common market among its members through the elimination of most trade barriers and the establishment of a common external trade policy. The treaty also provided for a common agricultural policy, which was established in 1962 to protect EEC farmers from agricultural imports. The first reduction in EEC internal tariffs was implemented in January 1959, and by July 1968 all internal tariffs had been removed. Between 1958 and 1968 trade among the EEC's members quadrupled in value. The term European Community also refers to the European Communities, which originally comprised the European Economic Community (EEC), the European Coal and Steel Community (ECSC; dissolved in 2002), and the European Atomic Energy Community (Euratom).

Politically, the EEC aimed to reduce tensions in the aftermath of World War II. In particular, it was hoped that integration would promote a lasting reconciliation of France and Germany, thereby reducing the potential for war. EEC governance required political cooperation among its members through formal supranational institutions. These institutions included the Commission, which formulated and administered EEC policies; the Council of Ministers, which enacted legislation; the European Parliament, originally a strictly consultative body whose members were delegates from national parliaments (later they would be directly elected); and the European Court of Justice, which interpreted community law and arbitrated legal disputes.

Members revamped the organization several times in order to expand its policy-making powers and to revise its political structure. On July 1, 1967, the governing bodies of the EEC, ECSC, and Euratom were merged. Through the Single European Act, which entered into force in 1987, EEC members committed themselves to remove all remaining barriers to a common market by 1992. The act also gave the EEC formal control of community policies on the environment, research and technology, education, health, consumer protection, and other areas.

By the Maastricht Treaty (formally known as the Treaty on European Union; 1991), which went into force on November 1, 1993, the European Economic Community was renamed the European Community and was embedded into the European Union (EU) as the first of its three "pillars" (the second being a common foreign and security policy and the third being police and judicial cooperation in criminal matters). The treaty also provided the foundation for an economic and monetary union, which included the creation of a single currency, the euro. The Lisbon Treaty, ratified in November 2009, extensively amended the governing documents of the EU. With the treaty's entry into force on December 1, 2009, the name European Community as well as the "pillars" concept were eliminated.

streamlining the EU's processes and giving it a higher international profile—was rejected in a referendum in June 2008; that verdict, however, was reversed in a second referendum on October 2, 2009.

THE ROUGH ROAD TO PROSPERITY

It was also in 1973 that the Fianna Fáil government of Jack Lynch (taoiseach since 1966) was defeated by a Fine Gael–Labour coalition led by Liam Cosgrave. The worldwide oil crisis and recession of 1974–75 forced the imposition of deflationary economic policies, a wealth tax, and attempts to tax farmers' incomes. Lynch returned to power in 1977 when Fianna Fáil proposed an ambitious economic policy based on tax cuts and the creation of new enterprises through foreign borrowing. Despite a brief boom, serious economic problems had become evident by 1980. These included declining agricultural prices, rising prices for imported oil, only a small increase in output, and a rapidly growing population, nearly half of which was under age 25. Moreover, foreign borrowing increased, and unemployment and inflation rose steeply. Civil strife in Northern Ireland, leading to a revival of the IRA, exposed dissensions within Fianna Fáil and culminated in Lynch's sensational sacking of Charles Haughey and Neal Blaney from his government in May 1970 for allegedly organizing the illegal importation of arms for the IRA. But, even when the charges against Blaney were dropped and Haughey was acquitted, the tensions continued to corrode Lynch's authority.

The early 1980s were politically volatile. Although no clear majority emerged in the election of 1981, Garret FitzGerald became taoiseach in a Fine Gael–Labour coalition, ousting Haughey, who had succeeded Lynch as Fianna Fáil leader in 1979. The rivalry between the charismatic FitzGerald (a Francophile, social democrat, academic, economist, and proponent of conciliation with Northern Ireland) and the no-less-charismatic Haughey (an Anglophobic, talented, high-living, and opportunistic pragmatist whose reputation was ultimately destroyed by revelations of his corruption and massive indebtedness to wealthy businessmen and to Ireland's largest bank) dominated the politics of the 1980s. The major campaign issues of the era were economic policy, including the imposition of a wealth tax, and the removal of a constitutional ban on divorce. The budget of the coalition government was defeated in January 1982, and a general election in February returned Fianna Fáil and Haughey to power. The new government's tenure was short and uneasy. In the face of a large budget deficit, a program of severe public spending cuts was introduced. The government was defeated on a no-confidence vote in November, and another general election—the third in 18 months—followed. This time a Fine Gael–Labour coalition under the leadership of FitzGerald secured a working majority.

By the mid-1980s the economy was showing signs of improvement. Inflation was at its lowest level in nearly two decades, helped by lower oil prices. However, the budget deficit and high unemployment continued to pose problems. Emigration, a barometer of Irish economic ill health, again began to increase in the mid-1980s. The prolonged recession had once again brought to the surface doubts and anxieties about the future of the Irish state and its real independence.

The economic crises of the 1970s and '80s were mirrored by political upheavals. In February 1987 Fianna Fáil returned to power under Haughey but without an overall majority; FitzGerald resigned as leader of Fine Gael and was succeeded by Alan Dukes. The new Progressive Democrat party (PD), formed in December 1985 largely from Fianna Fáil dissidents under the leadership of Desmond O'Malley, made a strong showing. Following a decision in November 1986 to abandon its policy of refusing to contest Dáil elections, Sinn Féin, the political wing of the Provisional IRA (which had split from the old IRA over the use of force in Northern Ireland), stood on a socialist and pro-IRA platform but failed to win a seat.

In 1989 Haughey smashed the mold of Fianna Fáil's refusal to participate in interparty governments when he formed a coalition with the Progressive Democrats—the first of a series of coalitions that continuously governed Ireland for the next 20 years—and the new government embarked on a program of comprehensive public spending cuts. The austerity measures were successful, and by the early 1990s the country's economic position had improved considerably. Inflation was low; budget deficits were reduced; and the annual growth rate was averaging more than 5 percent. The economy continued to boom throughout the late 1990s, fueled by the high-technology sector, with unemployment dropping to historically low levels.

MARY ROBINSON

Mary Robinson (born Mary Teresa Winifred Bourke, May 21, 1944, Ballina, County Mayo, Ireland), was educated at Trinity College and King's Inns in Dublin and at Harvard University in the United States. She served at Trinity College (University of Dublin) as Reid Professor of penal legislation, constitutional and criminal law, and the law of evidence (1969–75) and lecturer in European Community law (1975–90). In 1988 she established (with her husband) at Trinity College the Irish Centre for European Law. A distinguished constitutional lawyer and a renowned supporter of human rights, she was elected to the Royal Irish Academy and was a member of the International Commission of Jurists in Geneva (1987–90). She sat in the Seanad (upper chamber of Parliament) for the Trinity College constituency (1969–89) and served as whip for the Labour Party until resigning from the party over the Anglo-Irish Agreement of 1985, which she felt ignored unionist objections. She was also a member of the Dublin City Council (1979–83) and ran unsuccessfully in 1977 and 1981 for Dublin parliamentary constituencies.

Nominated by the Labour Party and supported by the Green Party and the Workers' Party, Robinson became Ireland's first woman president in 1990 by mobilizing a liberal constituency and merging it with a more conservative constituency opposed to the Fianna Fáil party. As president, Robinson adopted a much more prominent role than her predecessors, and she did much to

Mary Robinson, 2012. AFP/Getty Images

communicate a more modern image of Ireland. Strongly committed to human rights, she was the first head of state to visit Somalia after it suffered from civil war and famine in 1992 and the first to visit Rwanda after the genocide in that country in 1994. Shortly before her term as president expired, she took up the post of UNHCHR. As high commissioner, Robinson changed the priorities of her office to emphasize the promotion of human rights at the national and regional levels; she was the first UNHCHR to visit China, and she also helped to improve the monitoring of human rights in Kosovo. In 2001 Robinson served as secretary-general of the World Conference against Racism, Racial Discrimination, Xenophobia and Related Intolerance, held in Durban, South Africa. In 1998 she was elected chancellor of Trinity College.

After leaving her post at the UN, Robinson founded the nongovernmental organization Realizing Rights: The Ethical Globalization Initiative, in 2002. Its central concerns included equitable international trade, access to health care, migration, women's leadership, and corporate responsibility. She was also a founding member of the Council of Women World Leaders, served as honorary president of Oxfam International (a private organization that provides relief and development aid to impoverished or disaster-stricken communities worldwide), and was a member of the Club of Madrid (which promotes democracy). In 2004 Amnesty International awarded her its Ambassador of Conscience award for her human rights work. Her other honours include the U.S. Presidential Medal of Freedom (2009).

In 1990 Mary Robinson became the republic's first woman president. The election of a candidate with socialist and feminist sympathies was regarded as a watershed in Irish political life, reflecting the changes taking place in Irish society. Haughey was ousted in 1992 as leader of Fianna Fáil and as taoiseach by Albert Reynolds. A Fianna Fáil–Labour coalition came to power after the 1992 general election but collapsed in 1994. Another coalition, consisting of members of the Fine Gael, Labour, and Democratic Left parties, then took office, with Fine Gael leader John Bruton as taoiseach. The Bruton government lasted until the general election of June 1997, after which Fianna Fáil formed a new coalition with party leader Bertie Ahern as taoiseach.

In October Mary McAleese was elected president, the first Irish president from Northern Ireland (she was reelected in 2004). In 2002 Fianna Fáil formed yet another coalition government with the Progressive Democrats, headed again by Ahern. Although dogged by criticism through much of his tenure, Ahern capitalized on his personal popularity to lead Fianna Fáil to another election victory in 2007, and he formed yet another coalition government. Ahern's government continued to be dogged by an ongoing investigation (by the Tribunal of Inquiry into Certain Planning Matters & Payments [better known as the Mahon Tribunal]) of alleged payments by land developers to politicians to influence zoning decisions in and around Dublin during Ahern's tenure as finance minister in the early 1990s. In May 2008, as implications of Ahern's personal involvement in the scandal and allegations of past financial improprieties mounted, Ahern resigned as taoiseach.

THE DEBT CRISIS

His successor, Brian Cowen, was pitched headlong into Ireland's worst economic crisis since Fianna Fáil first came to power in 1932. Although this was partly due to the vulnerability of a small economy to the impact of the global financial crisis then afflicting much of the world, it was compounded by overexpenditure on public service pay and by the necessity to establish a National Asset Management Agency (NAMA) to bail out the insolvent Irish banks, which had persisted in making grotesquely extravagant and imprudent loans to property developers. The burden of rescuing the banks dramatically escalated the national deficit. So strained were Ireland's resources that in November 2010—even after proposing income tax hikes and reductions in services—the government was compelled to accept a bailout of more than $100 billion from the EU, the International Monetary Fund, and countries offering bilateral aid. In response to these developments, the Green Party, the junior partner in the ruling coalition with Fianna Fáil, called for early elections in January 2011. The unpopularity of the austerity measures required to meet the conditions of the loan, along with rumours of ethical impropriety, led to a challenge of Cowen's leadership of Fianna Fáil in mid-January 2011. He survived the leadership vote. But in a dizzying sequence of events that followed, Cowen called for an election to be held on March 11, then resigned as Fianna Fáil's leader, but remained on as a caretaker taoiseach, only to witness the withdrawal of the Green Party from the ruling coalition, with the likely consequence of an even earlier election.

At the end of January the Oireachtas (parliament) passed a finance bill that met the requirements of the IMF-EU bailout by raising taxes and cutting spending in an attempt to reduce the Irish deficit by $20.5 billion over the next four years. Following passage, Cowen officially called for elections to be held on February 25. In the event, Fianna Fáil—which was widely blamed for the country's financial troubles and for the unpopular bailout—took its worst drubbing at the polls in some 80 years, capturing only 20 seats in the Dáil. Meanwhile, Fine Gael nearly became the first party since 1977 to win an outright majority, winning 76 seats, the most in its history. Ultimately it formed a coalition government with the Labour Party. Fine Gael's leader, Enda Kenny, whose stature and popularity rose throughout the short election campaign, became taoiseach, while Labour's leader, Eamon Gilmore, assumed the post of *tánaiste* (deputy prime minister)

In mid-May Queen Elizabeth II undertook a four-day visit to Ireland, becoming both the first British monarch to visit the country in 100 years and the first to visit it since it had become an independent republic.

In October the Labour Party's Michael D. Higgins—a longtime member of the Dáil, a poet, and a former sociology professor—was elected to be McAleese's successor as president, emerging from a crowded field that included Sinn Féin's Martin McGuinness (who stepped down as deputy first minister of Northern Ireland to run).

In March 2012 Ireland's political culture was rocked by the release of the final report of the Mahon Tribunal, the country's longest-running public inquiry. The report concluded not only that former taoiseach Ahern had not been truthful in his testimony to the tribunal regarding his finances but also that every level of Irish political life had been affected by corruption tied to the scandal.

While Greece experienced widespread backlash against the austerity measures suggested by the IMF and the European Central Bank, Ireland was held up as a model of compliance. Although household spending continued to decline, consumer confidence improved as the IMF reported that Ireland had entered a period of modest economic recovery. Markets reacted negatively in late March 2012, however, when Kenny announced that he would put the EU's newly forged pact on fiscal discipline to a popular vote. Access to further bailout funds hinged on the approval of the treaty, and Kenny's government came out strongly in support of it. Although turnout for the May 31, 2012, referendum was low, voters approved the measure by a comfortable margin.

SOCIAL AND RELIGIOUS CHANGES

The close relationship between the Irish republic and the Roman Catholic Church was highlighted by the visit of Pope John Paul II to Ireland in 1979, the first visit there by a reigning pontiff. But the fraying of that relationship, signaled in the 1960s and '70s by a collapse in vocations to the priesthood and a decline in attendance at mass, continued in the 1980s and '90s. The clause in the 1937 constitution acknowledging the special position of the Roman Catholic Church was removed in 1972. (Among Ireland's most prominent non-Catholic politicians were a Jewish father and son, Robert and Ben Briscoe, both of whom served in the Dáil and as lord mayors of Dublin. Robert Briscoe was also a founding member of Fianna Fáil.) In 1983 the conservative resistance of Catholic pressure groups resulted in a referendum on a draft constitutional amendment reinforcing the republic's existing ban on abortion. After a divisive campaign, with barely a majority of the electorate voting in the referendum, voters approved the amendment.

In 1985 the church vainly opposed the government's liberalization of legislation concerning contraception. Church-state relations were tested again the following year when a referendum to remove the constitutional ban against divorce was defeated. A second referendum on abortion, which strengthened the existing antiabortion law but enabled women to travel overseas to obtain an abortion, was approved in 1992. Another referendum to lift the ban on divorce was held in 1995 and was passed by only a small majority; it went into effect in 1997. In 1992 the church was rocked by the first of a series of scandals when the bishop of Galway, Eamon Casey, resigned after it was discovered that he was the father of a teenage son. In 1995 controversy over the extradition to Northern Ireland of a pedophile priest, Brendan Smyth, brought down the Irish government. In 1999 the government announced the establishment of a commission to investigate the abuse that had been widespread until the 1970s in industrial and reformatory schools. Similar government commissions of inquiry conducted during the next decade culminated in the publication of the Murphy Report in 2009 (which reached devastating conclusions on the extent of concealment of priestly pedophilia in the Dublin archdiocese), in multiple episcopal resignations, in Pope Benedict XVI's summoning the Irish hierarchy to Rome, and, on March 20, 2010, in a papal letter apologizing to all victims of Catholic clerical sex abuse and announcing a formal Vatican investigation of Irish dioceses, seminaries,

BLOODY SUNDAY

Bloody Sunday began as a peaceful—but illegal—demonstration in Londonderry (Derry), Northern Ireland, on Sunday, January 30, 1972, by some 10,000 people organized by the Northern Ireland Civil Rights Association in opposition to the British government's policy of interning suspected IRA members without trial. When some of the demonstrators were confronted by soldiers and began pelting them with projectiles, the British troops responded by firing rubber bullets and a water cannon. Further violence erupted when the army began arresting demonstrators. Who had fired the first shot long remained a point of contention. The British army maintained that it had fired only after being fired upon; the Roman Catholic community contended that the soldiers had opened fire on unarmed protesters. After less than 30 minutes of shooting, 13 marchers lay dead. Ultimately, the Saville Report, issued in 2010, found that the first shot in the vicinity of the march had been fired by the British army and that, though there was some firing by republican paramilitaries, it did not provide any justification for the shooting of civilians.

British troops search Irish civilians on the day of the Bloody Sunday massacre, Derry (Londonderry), Northern Ireland, January 30, 1972. Popperfoto/Getty Images

and religious orders affected by the scandal.

RELATIONS WITH NORTHERN IRELAND

In 1957 the Irish government introduced internment without trial in response to an IRA campaign of attacks on British army and customs posts along the border with Northern Ireland that had begun in 1956 and lasted until 1962. An attempt to ease cross-border tensions was made in 1965, when Lemass exchanged visits with Terence O'Neill, Northern Ireland's prime minister.

The Irish government was increasingly preoccupied by the continuing violence in Northern Ireland that had first erupted in 1969. Lynch's dismissal of two of his ministers in 1970 following an attempt to import arms for use in Northern Ireland paved the way for a consensual approach, with all major parties increasingly committed to cooperating with the British government in seeking a peaceful resolution. Thus, Lynch's government supported the British government's suspension of the Northern Ireland parliament and government and the introduction of direct rule from Westminster in March 1972.

In December 1973, after the establishment of a power-sharing executive (composed of nationalists as well as unionists) in Northern Ireland, Liam Cosgrave's government participated in talks with Edward Heath, prime minister of Britain, and the power-sharing executive, resulting in the Sunningdale Agreement. This accord recognized that Northern Ireland's relationship with Britain could not be changed without the agreement of a majority of its population, and it provided for the establishment of a Council of Ireland composed of members from both the Dáil and the Northern Ireland assembly. But direct rule was reimposed when that agreement collapsed in May 1974 because of a general strike inspired by unionist opponents of power-sharing.

Although the republic experienced nothing like the scale of the continuing violence in Northern Ireland, there were a number of serious terrorist incidents. On May 17, 1974, three car bombs in Dublin and one in Monaghan caused an eventual death toll of 33 (the largest number killed on any one day since the violence began in 1970). The IRA's murder of the British ambassador in Dublin in 1976 led to a state of emergency and the unpopular measure of strengthening emergency-powers legislation, and the assassination at his holiday home in Sligo of Earl Louis Mountbatten of Burma (Britain's last viceroy in India) by the IRA in 1979 further intensified opposition to terrorism.

In 1981 FitzGerald launched a constitutional crusade to make the reunification of Ireland more attractive to Northern Ireland's Protestants. At the end of the year, the Irish and British governments set up an Anglo-Irish intergovernmental council to discuss matters of common concern, especially security. In 1984 the report of the New Ireland Forum—a discussion group that included representatives of political parties in Ireland and Northern Ireland—set out three possible frameworks for political development in Ireland: a unitary state, a federal state, and joint sovereignty. Fianna Fáil preferred a unitary state, which Fine Gael and Labour regarded as unrealistic; they preferred the federal option. In November 1985 at Hillsborough in Northern Ireland, Ireland and Britain again agreed that any change in the status of Northern Ireland would come about only with the consent of the majority of the people of Northern Ireland, and an intergovernmental conference was established to deal with political, security, and legal relations between the two parts of the island.

Despite Fianna Fáil's initial criticism of the 1985 Anglo-Irish Agreement, the Haughey government worked the agreement. Contacts between the Irish and British governments continued after February 1987 within the formal structure of the intergovernmental conference. Fears that the violence in Northern Ireland would spill into Ireland as a consequence of closer Anglo-Irish cooperation in the wake of the agreement proved unfounded.

In 1993 the Irish and British governments signed a joint peace initiative (the Downing Street Declaration), in which they pledged to seek mutually agreeable political structures in Northern Ireland and between the two islands. In 1994 the IRA declared a cease-fire, and for the next 18 months there was considerable optimism that a new period of political cooperation between north and south had been inaugurated. The cease-fire collapsed in 1996, however, and the IRA resumed its bombing campaign.

In 1998 the taoiseach, Bertie Ahern, played an important role in brokering the Good Friday Agreement (Belfast Agreement), which would create a Northern Ireland Assembly, establish north-south political structures, and amend Ireland's 1937 constitution by removing from it the de jure claim to Northern Ireland. On May 22, 1998, the agreement was approved by 94 percent of voters in Ireland and by 71 percent in Northern Ireland. With the establishment of the power-sharing assembly, the Irish government continued to remain active in promoting peace and economic development in Northern Ireland. The Northern Ireland Assembly's assumption of power was halting, however, and was suspended intermittently, largely in response to the failure of the paramilitary forces to fully decommission and disarm. But in May 2007, following another round of new elections to the Northern Ireland Assembly and two years after the IRA's abandonment of armed struggle, power sharing became a reality in Northern Ireland.

CONCLUSION

It is helpful to remember that the emergence of Ireland as an independent country is a fairly recent phenomenon. From the early 17th century, Ireland effectively was an English colony, and from 1800 to 1922 it was an integral part of the United Kingdom. The Anglo-Irish Treaty of 1921 established the Irish Free State as a self-governing dominion of the British Empire, but real independence did not come until 1937. Yet Ireland remained a member of the British Commonwealth until 1948.

Since then, Ireland has become integrated with the rest of western Europe, joining the European Union in 1987, but its journey toward the 21st century was filled with challenges, notably economic hardships and the perennial conflict in Northern Ireland. The Irish proved themselves to be up to those challenges, however, as they reinvented and reinvigorated their economy in the 1990s as the technology-driven Celtic Tiger. Not only that, but the Irish government played a pivotal role in the series of agreements that led to a cessation of fighting in the north and, by the early 21st century, to power-sharing rule among factions in Northern Ireland that had for so long seemed as if they would never find common ground. The future of Ireland looked bright, but then the economic and financial collapse of 2008 hit hard. Reeling, Ireland required a bailout from the EU and the IMF; austerity became the guiding policy. But if history has shown anything about the Irish people, it is that they can take a punch, come back swinging, and ultimately finish a bout with hands aloft in victory.

ADJUTANT Military staff officer who assists the commanding officer and is responsible especially for correspondence.

ANGLICAN Of or relating to the established episcopal Church of England and churches of similar faith and order in communion with it.

ASPHODEL Any of several flowering plants belonging to the lily family.

BESTIALITY The condition or status of a lower animal.

BISHOPRIC The office of bishop. (Similarly, an archbishopric is the office of an archbishop.)

BOG Wet, spongy ground.

BOOK OF KELLS Illuminated manuscript version of the four Gospels, from the late 8th–early 9th century.

CELT Member of a division of the early central-European peoples distributed from the British Isles and Spain to Asia Minor.

CHANCERY Record office for public archives or those of ecclesiastical, legal, or diplomatic proceedings; the office of the "great seal of the king used in Ireland."

CIVIL LAW Body of law developed from Roman law and used in continental Europe and most former colonies of European nations, including the province of Quebec and the U.S. state of Louisiana.

COTERMINOUS Having the same or coincident boundaries.

DIOCESE The territorial jurisdiction of a bishop. (Similarly, an archdiocese is the territorial jurisdiction of an archbishop.)

DRACONIAN Cruel; severe.

DUTY-FREE Without payment of customs duties, as in a duty-free shop at an airport.

ECCLESIASTICAL Of or relating to a church, especially as an established institution.

EQUABLE Marked by lack of variation or change.

ESTUARY Water passage where the tide meets a river current, especially an arm of the sea at the lower end of a river.

EXCHEQUER Department or office of state in medieval England charged with the collection and management of the royal revenue and judicial determination of all revenue causes.

FLEABANE Any of various composite plants that were once believed to drive away fleas.

FORENSIC Argumentative; rhetorical.

GOIDELIC One of two groups of the modern Celtic languages; the group includes Irish, Manx, and Scottish Gaelic.

HEGEMONY Preponderant influence or authority over others; domination.

HIBERNIAN Of, relating to, or characteristic of Ireland or the Irish. (Though they never visited in person, it was the Romans who dubbed Ireland Hibernia, meaning land of winter.)

HIGHLANDS Elevated or mountainous land.

LEPRECHAUN Mischievous elf of Irish folklore usually believed to reveal the hiding place of treasure if caught.

LIMITED LIABILITY Condition under which the loss that an owner (shareholder) of a business firm may incur is limited to the amount of capital invested by him or her in the business and does not extend to personal assets.

MAGNATE Person of rank, power, influence, or distinction often in a specified area.

MARITIME Of, relating to, or bordering on the sea.

OGHAM Alphabetic system of 5th- and 6th-century Irish in which an alphabet of 20 letters is represented by notches for vowels and lines for consonants and which is known principally from inscriptions cut on the edges of rough standing tombstones.

ORANGE ORDER Irish Protestant and political society, named for the Protestant William of Orange, who, as King William III of Great Britain, had defeated the Roman Catholic King James II. The society was formed in 1795 to maintain the Protestant ascendancy in Ireland in the face of rising demands for Catholic Emancipation. Also known as Orangemen.

PASTURAGE Pasture.

PATRON SAINT Saint to whom a person, society, church, or place is dedicated.

PEAT Dark brown or blackish material that is the remains of plants partly decayed in water and is sometimes dug up and dried for use as fuel.

PEER Member of one of the five ranks of the British nobility.

PHONOLOGY Science of speech sounds including especially the history and theory of sound changes in a language or in two or more related languages.

PRELATE High-ranking member of the clergy (as a bishop).

PRESBYTERY Part of a church reserved for the officiating clergy.

PRETENDER TO THE THRONE Claimant to a throne who is held to have no just title.

PRIMOGENITURE Exclusive right of inheritance belonging to the eldest son.

PROMULGATE Proclaim; declare.

PROSAIC Dull, ordinary, or uninteresting.

RESTORATION Following the death of Oliver Cromwell (1658), the reestablishment of the monarchy in England in 1660 under Charles II.

SANDHI Modification of the sound of a word or a part of a word in various situations. (For instance, compare the sound of "ed" in glazed and wanted.)

SEDITIOUS Disposed to arouse or take part in secession.

SINN FÉIN Nationalist political party in Ireland; the political wing of the Irish Republican Army (IRA).

SOBRIQUET Nickname.

STOAT Short-tailed weasel.

SUFFRAGE The right to vote.

SYNOD Ecclesiastical governing or advisory council.

TILLAGE Farming.

TUATHA Kingdoms, clans.

UILLEANN PIPES Irish bagpipe with air supplied by a bellows held under and worked by the elbow.

UNHCHR The United Nations High Commissioner for Human Rights. Appointed by the secretary-general in a regular rotation of geographic regions and approved by the General Assembly, the UNHCHR serves a fixed term of four years with the possibility of renewal for an additional four-year term.

VERNACULAR Of, relating to, or using ordinary, especially spoken, language.

WATTLE Fabrication of poles interwoven with slender branches, withes, or reeds and used formerly in building especially.

WIN, PLACE, OR SHOW Betting terminology in horseracing; the horse that wins comes in first, that which places comes in second, and that which shows comes in third.

WORLD TRADE ORGANIZATION International organization that helps nations trade their goods and services with one another. There are currently about 150 member countries in the WTO.

ZOOMORPHIC Having the form or attributes of an animal.

Bibliography

GEOGRAPHY

Informative overviews include James Gleason and Deirdre Purcell, *Contemplating Ireland* (2000); and Sean Kay, *Celtic Revival?: The Rise, Fall, and Renewal of Global Ireland* (2011). The geography of Ireland is explored in the journal *Irish Geography*, published three times annually by the Geographical Society of Ireland. Studies of Irish politics and culture include Robert Savage (ed.), *Ireland in the New Century: Politics, Culture, and Identity* (2003); and Bill Kissane, *Explaining Irish Democracy* (2002). Social, environmental, and economic aspects of Ireland are the subject of R.W.G. Carter and A.J. Parker (eds.), *Ireland* (1989). F.H.A. Aalen, Kevin Whelan, and Matthew Stout (eds.), *Atlas of the Irish Rural Landscape*, 2nd ed., rev. and expanded (2011), addresses such topics as archaeology, field and settlement patterns, houses, villages and small towns, monuments, roads, canals, railways, mills, mines, and handball alleys. A beautifully illustrated overview of the historical development of the Irish language is Máirtín Ó Murchú, *The Irish Language* (1985). The environment, population patterns, political geography, and economic planning are explored in James H. Johnson, *The Human Geography of Ireland* (1994). The economy is discussed in Cormac Ó Gráda, *Ireland: A New Economic History, 1780–1939* (1994); and J.W. O'Hagan (ed.), *The Economy of Ireland: Policy and Performance of a Small European Country* (1995).

Irish culture over the centuries is covered in Brian De Breffny (ed.), *The Irish World: The Art and Culture of the Irish People* (1977, reissued 2000); Robin Flower, *The Irish Tradition* (1947, reissued 1994), a review of Gaelic Ireland's contribution to western European culture; Marjorie Howes, *Colonial Crossings: Figures in Irish Literary History* (2006); E. Estyn Evans, *Irish Folk Ways* (1957, reissued 1988); Robert Savage, *A Loss of Innocence?: Television and Irish Society, 1962–70* (2010); and Liam Harte and Michael Parker (eds.), *Contemporary Irish Fictions: Themes, Tropes, Theories* (2000).

HISTORY

Informative surveys of Ireland's history include James McGuire and James Quinn (eds.), *Dictionary of Irish Biography: From the Earliest Times to the Year 2002*, 9 vol. (2009); John O'Beirne Ranelagh, *A Short History of Ireland*, 3rd ed. (2012); S.J. Connolly (ed.), *The Oxford Companion to Irish History*, 2nd ed. (2002); Ruth Dudley Edwards and Bridget Hourican, *An Atlas of Irish History*, 3rd ed. (2005); R.F. Foster, *Modern Ireland, 1600–1972* (1988); and A.T.Q. Stewart, *The Narrow Ground: The Roots of Conflict in Ulster*, rev. ed. (1989, reissued 1993).

Modern Ireland under British rule in the 17th–19th centuries is the subject of Ciran Brady and Jane Ohlmeyer (eds.), *British Interventions in Early Modern Ireland* (2004); Micheál Ó Siochru, *God's Executioner: Oliver Cromwell and the Conquest of Ireland* (2008); Jane Ohlmeyer (ed.), *Ireland from Independence to Occupation, 1641–1660* (1995, reissued 2002); Éamonn Ó Ciardha, *Ireland and the Jacobite Cause, 1685–1766* (2002); Thomas Bartlett, *The Fall and Rise of the Irish Nation: The Catholic Question, 1690–1830* (1992); and S.J. Connolly, *Priests and People in Pre-Famine Ireland, 1780–1845* (1982, reissued 2001). Oliver MacDonagh, *O'Connell: The Life of Daniel O'Connell, 1775–1847* (1991); and Patrick M. Geoghegan, *King Dan: The Rise of Daniel O'Connell, 1775–1829* (2008), are reflections on the life of Daniel O'Connell. John Crowley, William J. Smyth, and Mike Murphy (eds.), *Atlas of the Great Irish Famine* (2012), and R. Dudley Edwards and T. Desmond Williams (eds.), *The Great Famine: Studies in Irish History, 1845–52* (1956, reissued 1994), discuss one of the worst disasters that influenced the course of Irish history. Important monographs on 19th-century Irish politics include R.V. Comerford, *The Fenians in Context: Irish Politics and Society, 1848–82* (1985, reissued 1998); Tom Garvin, *Nationalist Revolutionaries in Ireland, 1858–1928* (1987); and F.S.L. Lyons, *Charles Stewart Parnell* (1977, reissued 1991).

Alvin Jackson, *Ireland 1798–1998* (1999), considers the 19th and 20th centuries. More-specific topics focused primarily on the 20th century are examined in J.R. Hill (ed.), *Ireland, 1921–1984* (2003); Ronan Fanning, *Independent Ireland* (1983); Diarmaid Ferriter, *The Transformation of Ireland, 1900–2000* (2004); Patrick Maume, *The Long Gestation: Irish Nationalist Life, 1891–1918* (1999); A.T.Q. Stewart, *The Ulster Crisis* (1967, reissued 1997); Charles Townshend, *Easter 1916: The Irish Rebellion* (2005); Michael Laffan, *The Partition of Ireland, 1911–25* (1983), and *The Resurrection of Ireland: The Sinn Féin Party, 1916–1923* (1999); Peter Hart, *Mick: The Real Michael Collins* (2005); Michael Hopkinson, *Green Against Green: The Irish Civil War* (1988, reissued 2004); Nicholas Mansergh, *The Unresolved Question: The Anglo-Irish Settlement and Its Undoing, 1912–72* (1991); Michael Kennedy, *Division and Consensus: The Politics of Cross-Border Relations in Ireland, 1925–1969* (2000); Liam Kennedy, *The Modern Industrialisation of Ireland, 1940–1988* (1989); and J. Bowyer Bell, *The Irish Troubles: A Generation of Violence, 1967–1992* (1993). *The flag of Ireland.*

INDEX